Nautical Antiques
& Collectables

**Contemporary photograph taken from the flying bridge of the
Cunard liner *Mauretania***

The *Mauretania* was built by Messrs Swan, Hunter & Wigham Richardson & Co. Ltd, Newcastle
in 1907.
Photographic silver print, English, c.1907, 30 x 30cm (12 x 8in)

Nautical Antiques & Collectables

Jon Baddeley

SOTHEBY'S PUBLICATIONS

First published in 1993 by Sotheby's Publications
an imprint of Philip Wilson Publishers Ltd
26 Litchfield Street
London WC2H 9NJ

ISBN 0 85667 394 3

LC 92-063278

Designed and typeset by Christopher Matthews and Ian Muggeridge
Printed in Great Britain by Jolly & Barber Printing Limited, Rugby,
Warwickshire

Contents

Introduction

ALTHOUGH much has been published over the last twenty years on the subject of marine paintings, there is very little material available in the general field of decorative marine works of art. Many, very informative books exist on subjects such as scrimshaw and figureheads, however, there is a growing number of collectors who are interested in the broader aspects of marine artefacts and collect across all such disciplines, from paintings to models and instruments.

Above all, collecting should be a fun pastime, with all the prize pieces in a collection having a story to tell, not only about their use and construction, but on their acquisition. The chase is certainly an important part of collecting and a serious collector will use the services of a specialist dealer or auction house, as well as keeping abreast of small antique fairs and markets. There are still many pieces to be found and collectors are often able to identify an item which has been overlooked by the dealer or specialist. Such finds happen on a regular basis and this stimulates the keen collector to maintain a continual search.

There are many museums worldwide specializing in marine items, and some of these are listed in the final chapters of this book. They range from small local museums to national collections of great repute and are all of interest to an enthusiast and can frequently help in identifying an unknown find. The curators themselves are often more than willing to help with research and advise on conservation.

Finally, there is the question of price and of how much to pay. In my twenty years experience of selling such a commodity, I have yet to find a collector who regretted paying a high price at auction for a particular rare and important piece. However, there are many disappointed clients who stopped bidding and lost the chance forever of acquiring another addition to their collection.

The golden rules are, in my opinion, to buy from a respected individual or company; to obtain a full descriptive invoice and to buy the rarest and the best quality you can afford. Buying purely for investment should be avoided, since fashions change and prices rise and fall due to many financial and political fluctuations. While an expensive item will always show a return in the long term, it is impossible to place a price on years of enjoyment a piece will give to the owner during this period.

Acknowledgements

I am indebted to the many collectors who have kindly allowed me access to their collections and freely given of their specialist knowledge. They have been the prime source for the majority of the information contained within this book.

In addition, I am greatly indebted to the acknowledged experts in their fields for reading and correcting the proofs. Their input has been much appreciated and their background of either having worked at, or being currently employed by, the National Maritime Museum at Greenwich, makes them more qualified to assist with the factual content. They are Dr John Graves, John Munday and Anthony Turner.

My present and past colleagues at Sotheby's continue to impress me with the depth and breadth of their knowledge. In particular Michael Naxton, who, although more known for his expertise in the areas of coins and medals, has, without doubt, an in-depth knowledge and enthusiasm for all things marine.

Tom Rose of Christie's and Patrick Bogue of Onslow's have kindly given me access to their photographic files, as have the National Maritime Museum, Beken of Cowes and, of course, Sotheby's.

In particular I would like to thank, for their exceptional input, Nina Giebel who, as photographer with the Sotheby's Collectors' departmental team for the past ten years, has composed and shot many thousands of items, each with a care and attention to detail and design unsurpassed in my experience of producing hundreds of auction catalogues. Also my collegue, Patricia Lawrence, who made order out of a somewhat chaotic working environment, and worked exceedingly hard at collecting and editing the text that arrived spasmodically and uncorrected from my word processor.

Finally, I am greatly indebted to Kerry, without whose continual support and help this project could not have been completed.

Jon Baddeley

Ship Models

THE ART of making ship and boat models can be traced back to many ancient civilizations. However, it was not until the seventeenth century that fairly accurate scale models began to be produced in Europe for use as working, three dimensional plans by shipwrights.

In general, ship and boat models fall into four distinct categories: those made as part of the process of shipbuilding and boat-building; those constructed professionally for commercial promotion; those built by sailors, either for recreational, votive or commercial purposes; and finally modern, hobby-made models.

Shipbuilding models

One of the foremost English shipwrights in the early seventeenth century was Phineas Pett (1570-1647), and recorded in his autobiography are several references to the models he either made himself, or ordered to be made as designs for the ships he built.

Pett worked for the Master Shipwright, Mathew Baker, until 1596, at which time he joined forces with his brother, Joseph, another shipwright. His earliest reference to a model is in 1596, when he recorded, 'and was afterwards employed by my brother at Limehouse, upon a small model for the Lord Treasurer, William Cecil, Lord Burghley'. There is no other record of this model, and unfortunately it does not form part of the fabulous collection of fine and decorative art at Burghley House in Lincolnshire.

In March 1601, Pett was appointed as assistant to the Master Shipwright at Chatham dockyard, where he gained favour by fitting out the fleet in the remarkable period of only six weeks. He was commissioned by Lord Howard, the Lord Admiral, to make a miniature ship for the King's elder son, Prince Henry, which he completed in March 1604. It was apparently a great success, since Pett was sworn as the Prince's servant and made Captain of the little vessel. In 1607, Pett made a further model called the *Prince Royal*:

After my settling at Woolwich, I began a curious model for the Prince my Master, most part where-off, I wrought with my own hands; which being most fairly garnished with carving and painting, and placed in a frame, arched, covered, and curtained with crimson taffety, was, the 10th day of November by me presented to the Lord High Admiral at his lodging at Whitehall. His Lordship well approving of it, after I had supped with his Honour that night, gave me commandment to carry the same to Richmond where the Prince, my master, then lay ... His majesty was exceedingly delighted with the sight of the model and spent some time in questioning me divers material things concerning the same, and demanding whether I would build the Great Ship in all points like to the same, for I will (said his Majesty) compare them together when she shall be finished.

The full-sized *Prince Royal* was built by Phineas Pett and launched at Woolwich in 1610, but, sadly, there is no record of the present whereabouts of these two models.

One of the largest and most lavishly decorated ships built in the seventeenth century was

Stern view of a Navy Board model of a 50-gun ship

Although this model depicts an unnamed vessel, it can be dated with a degree of accuracy by measuring its dimensions and comparing these with contemporary plans. Built to a scale of 1:64, the model could not represent vessels built before 1719 or after 1733.

Boxwood, brass, ivory and ebonized wood, English, c.1725,
78 x 23 x 14.5cm (30¾ x 9 x 7¾in)

the famous *Royal Sovereign*, or *Sovereign of the Seas*, commissioned by Charles I and built by Peter Pett under the supervision of his father, Phineas. At a time when a ship of forty guns cost in the region of £6,000, the *Royal Sovereign* cost approximately £65,000.

That the model of the *Royal Sovereign* undoubtedly had fantastic decorative appeal, is recorded by a certain Peter Munday, who travelled to Woolwich to see the ship being built. During that time he visited Peter Pett's house:

where wee sawe the Moddel or Molde of the said shippe, which was shewne unto his Majestie before he begun her. The said Modele was of admiral Workemanshipp, curiouslye painted and guilte, with azur and gold, soe contrived that every timber in her might be seene and left open and unplanked for that purpose, very neate and delightsome. There were also the moddels of divers other shippes lately built, but nothing to compare with the former.

Travels of Peter Munday, Hakluyt Society, Second Series, Vol XVL

This is the earliest record of a model being built with an unplanked hull in order to show details of the internal construction. However, there is no reason to suppose that Pett's earlier models were not similarly constructed.

Navy Board models

Today, Navy Board or Admiralty models are certainly the most expensive and the most highly-prized examples of historic ship models in any private or public collection. These extraordinary models portray, in perfect detail, the form and often complex structure of naval ships from the seventeenth and eighteenth centuries, using high-grade materials and sometimes displaying, with exquisite accuracy, the ship's external decorations and internal furnishings. Although contemporary paintings and plans give a good idea of how a full-rigged ship looked during this period, these three dimensional models give a unique insight into the naval architecture and decorations of their day.

The distinctive characteristic of such models is the exposed framing of the hull and the internal details visible below the gunwales, where the hull and deck are left partially un-planked. This framing is invariably stylized and models showing accurately depicted framing are rare. They were generally built from fruitwood to a scale of 1:48 and normally unrigged, although a number appear to have been rigged at a later date. There are only two seventeenth-century models still in existence with contemporary rigging, one of which, dated 1710, forms part of the collection at the National Maritime Museum, Greenwich.

Why these models were originally built is uncertain. It has been suggested that they were submitted by the shipbuilder, together with a set of drawings, for inspection by the members of the Navy Board prior to the construction of the full-size ship. It is, however, surprising that Samuel Pepys, although making many references to ship models in his famous diary, did not mention their connection with ship design. Pepys himself, formed an important collection of ship models during his long tenure in office as Clerk of the Acts, and later as Secretary to the Admiralty. On his death in 1703, Pepys bequeathed the collection to his friend and former servant, William Hewer, and recommended that they should be 'Preserved for Publique Benifit'.

Unfortunately the history of the collection following this remains a mystery, and it can only be assumed that it was broken up and is now dispersed among many famous public and private collections.

In 1659, the English Master Shipwright, Francis Sheldon, went to work for a Swedish shipbuilders. By way of credentials he took with him a framed model of a warship he had built.

Following the signing of the treaty of the Peace of Roskilde with Denmark in 1659, the Swedish King, Charles XI, founded the naval base of Karlskrona at Blekinge, on the island of Trossö, for building warships. The models built there were declared an official collection by King Adolph Frederik and today form the basis of the Swedish Marine Museum at Karlskrona. In Copenhagen, the Royal Shipyard established a special design room in 1695 where model builders were able, for the first time, to work at their craft. Part of this collection can still be seen today at the Naval Warfare Museum at Copenhagen.

If these highly detailed models were not made as architectural pieces, it must be assumed that they were built on commission, perhaps as expensive gifts, for particular patrons and noblemen. This may account for the fact that so many Navy Board models do not depict specific vessels. Another suggestion is that they were fashioned at the same time as the ship itself, and used during the period of construction to demonstrate to the Surveyor of the Navy the progress of work, rather than endeavouring to portray this on the actual site of the shipyard.

No doubt many were made by the shipwrights themselves as an exquisite celebration of the full-size warships that left their yard for service in the Royal Navy. Whatever their original purpose, Navy Board models are today a unique record, in miniature, of the industrial technology of shipbuilding in the seventeenth and eighteenth centuries.

Admiralty model of a frigate on a slipway

High-quality materials were sometimes used by the Admiralty model-makers to enhance the visual attraction of their craft. This frigate is built with an ivory wheel, stanchions and blocks. The body of the ship, however, is made from boxwood. The mahogany base opens out to form a slipway down which the model can be made to travel.

Boxwood, ivory and mahogany, English, late 18th century, model 107cm (42in) long; slipway extended 219cm (86in) long

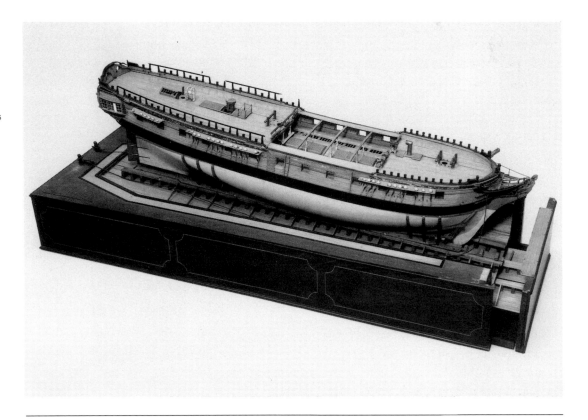

Admiralty model of the 70-gun ship-of-the-line H.M.S. *Edinburgh*

Constructed from fruitwood, this model is painted white below the waterline and is decorated with a gilded stern panel, carved with the British coat of arms, and bows with a typical rampant lion figurehead.

The model belonged to Richard Hampden, Treasurer of the Navy Board from 1718 to 1720, and it was one of the first to be constructed according to the new Establishment for naval ship design, laid down in 1719.

Fruitwood, English, 1721, 30.5 x 114 x 27cm (12 x 45 x 10½in)

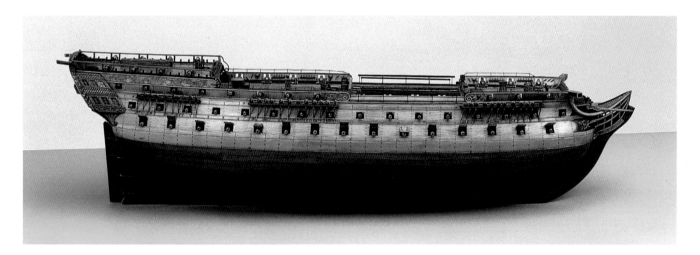

Model of the 92-gun ship-of-the-line H.M.S. *Canopus*

This boxwood and ivory model was constructed in France at the end of the 18th century and combines many of the finest features of the best Admiralty and prisoner-of-war ship models of the period. The stern is decorated with a carved boxwood coat of arms flanked by figures of mermaids, and the deck panels are applied with finely-carved acanthus leaf decoration.

The main deck illustration clearly shows the belaying rails and pins, the double wheel, companionways, guns on carriages and the stained ivory strakes along the side.

Originally named *Franklin*, the *Canopus* was built at Toulon in France in 1796, but was captured by the British and re-named at the Battle of the Nile. She saw service in the Mediterranean and home waters from 1803 until she was finally broken up in 1887.

Boxwood and ivory, French, late 18th century, 100cm (39in) long

Model of the 100-gun, first-rate ship-of-the-line *Royal George*, stern and figurehead details

One side of the model has been left unplanked to show the construction and interior fittings, while the starboard side is shown complete (left). The extraordinary attention to detail is demonstrated by the two stern gallery lanterns, the insides of which have been gilded and fitted with miniature model candles. The window glass has been made from mica, a mineral which, when cut wafer-thin, is a transparent laminate.

The figurehead (above) has been carved in great detail from a single piece of boxwood, with the royal coat of arms flanked by figures and horses. Just beyond the figurehead, the construction incorporates carved ivory with ebony and mother-of-pearl inlay.

The *Royal George* was launched on 1 February 1756, after spending ten years on the stocks and cost £54,664.

The model was made in 1772 at Deptford Dockyard for the personal use of King George III (then the Prince of Wales). It has subsequently been owned by several monarchs, including William IV, who presented it to Greenwich Hospital in 1830.

Boxwood, English, 1772, 140 x 44 x 34cm (55¼ x 17¼ x 13¼in)

Block and half-block models

During the eighteenth century, ship models were certainly made as designs for full-size ships, but there are surprisingly few recorded in public collections today. Their existence is confirmed, however, by an order from the Navy Board, dated 4 June 1716, to the Master Shipwrights of the Royal Dockyard stating, 'You are to prepare and send with your said draught, a solid or model'. This probably refers to a simple, painted model known as a 'block model', being all the ancient shipbuilders needed as a design to show the shape of the hull, gun port layout and other external features, rather than the highly-detailed Navy Board models.

The 'block' was constructed from layers of wood, the lines of which had been lifted from the plan and assembled 'bread-and-butter' fashion. The hull was then carved and planed to produce a smooth finish. Normally the decoration, gun port arrangement and other details were simply either painted on to the wood, or on to paper that was subsequently glued to the model, as opposed to specifically detailing the figures by carving them into the wood.

In comparison with naval ships, few block models of merchant ships were made during the eighteenth century, with the exception of those models of East India Company vessels which, due to their special service, were built along naval lines. Merchant ship models were used as designs to find the optimum cargo carrying capacity, combined with the speed and stability of the vessel. The model-maker carved a half-model of either the port or starboard side of the vessel, and then cut the model into sections at the intervals of the frames. These sections were then traced on to paper and subsequently enlarged to the actual size of the finished hull.

In America, a similar method was used for constructing fast merchant sailing ships and yachts. Rather than carving the model from a solid piece of wood, the hull was made from a number of boards placed horizontally and held together by pegs; the shape of the hull was then carved from this sandwich. The model could then be taken apart, each section being used as curves from which to draft the waterlines.

During the nineteenth century the half-block model was used as the intermediate stage between the plan and the building of the full-size vessel. This practice is still continued in some

Shipbuilder's half-block model of the barque *Torridon*

The model is set on to a mirrored surface, to give the impression of a complete ship, and is housed in an attractive mahogany bow-fronted glazed case. Built by Paul Hall & Co. of Aberdeen, the barque has a carved wood female figurehead and deck, with silver-plated fittings including capstan, ventilators, deck lights, hand rails and lifeboat on davits.

Mahogany and glass, Scottish, 1885, 51 x 207cm (20 x 81½in)

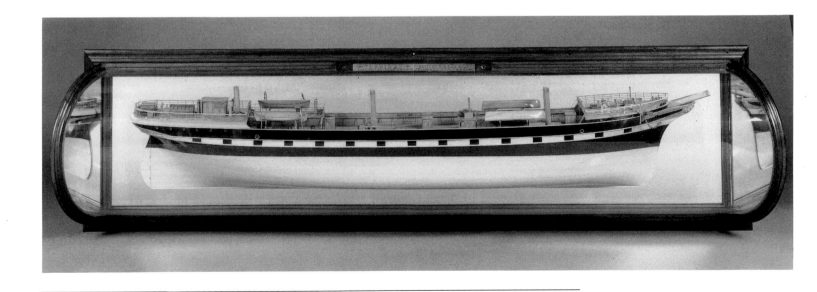

yards today. The more humble vessels only required small models, mounted on a wall plaque with, perhaps, the ship's name painted alongside. The more prestigious late nineteenth-century passenger and cargo vessels had painted hulls and simulated planked decking, with well-detailed fittings including handrails, deckhouses, winch gear, navigational lamps and lifeboats on davits. To facilitate their display, the models were sometimes mounted on a silvered mirror to give the impression of a full-hull model. Some of the most attractive half-blocks are those of pleasure and racing yachts which were built using a combination of light and dark woods in order to emphasize the various waterlines.

Display models

Shipbuilders' models were often used by builders or owners to advertise their business at commercial exhibitions and trade fairs. Such full models were obviously made to impress the public and were constructed with great attention to detail, using high-quality materials. In some instances two identical models would have been made of the same ship, one for the shipbuilder and the other for the shipowner. These passenger and cargo vessels were normally built to a scale of 1:48 and were presented in attractive glazed mahogany cases on stands, examples of which can still be seen today in the boardrooms and foyers of the larger shipping and marine insurance companies.

During the late nineteenth century such models were generally made in the dockyard workshops, or at small local model builders. The shipbuilders, Vickers Armstrong and John Brown, both had model workshops employing many technicians who produced some of the finest builders' models in the world. However, by the beginning of the twentieth century this had begun to change. A Northampton-based company called Bassett-Lowke set up a model engineering business, part of which was to provide the shipyards with models on a commission basis, but they did not seriously penetrate the market for manufacturing models for the large shipyards until after World War II.

In addition to supplying the shipyards, they also produced a wide range of display and working models for the general public, either to order, or available through their many retail outlets. They were also commissioned to make models promoting transatlantic travel, and these included the famous liners *France*, *Mauretania* and the ill-fated *Titanic*. In 1921, to meet growing demand, Bassett-Lowke founded an independent workshop, Ship Models Ltd, to concentrate on ship model production and to distance this from the thriving model train portion of their business empire. Using skilled craftsmen brought to Northampton from the Sunderland dockyards, and utilising impressive display cases, the new company quickly secured orders from the Blue Star Line, Royal Mail Steam Packet Company, Cunard and other shipping companies.

Bassett-Lowke also produced a series of miniature waterline models to a scale of 1:1200, which were popular as souvenirs with serving navy men. Made in die-cast white metal they included all types of warships, submarines and small auxiliary vessels, such as mine-sweepers and supply ships. The company also manufactured so-called 'pond-yachts' based along the lines of the famous J-class designs. These working sailing yachts proved ever popular with fathers and sons alike to sail on park ponds, and were made in considerable numbers until the outbreak of World War II.

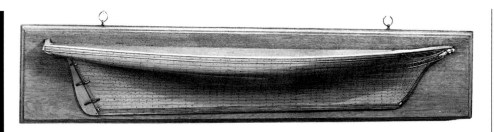

Shipbuilder's half-block model of the yacht *Kate*

Constructed from beechwood, the fine lines of this yacht are enhanced by the use of a planked hull and brass pins. The bow is decorated with a carved female figurehead, probably portraying *Kate*, but unusually made from bone rather than carved from wood.

Beechwood, English, second half of the 19th century, 97cm (38in) long

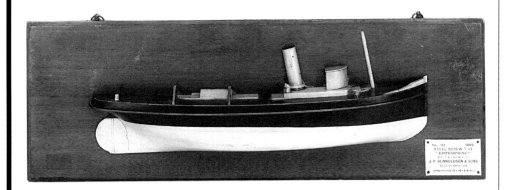

Shipbuilder's half-block model of the steam tug *Enterprise*

Many shipbuilders' models were made for public display and thus carried an ivory or brass plaque detailing the type of vessel, dimensions and the maker. This half-model has a plate engraved with the yard number, the date of construction and the dimensions. It also specifies that the vessel was built and fitted with an engine by J. P. Rennoldson & Sons of South Shields.

Mahogany and pine, English, 1899, 65cm (25½in) long

Shipbuilder's half-block model of the paddle-steamer *Precursor*

Builders' models of such vessels are quite rare, since the number of full-size paddle-steamers built, compared to screw propulsion ships, was small. Ocean-going paddle-steamers were subject to the disadvantages of broken paddle-wheels and shafts when the ship rolled in heavy seas, and their efficiency varied depending on how low the ship was in the water when it was moving. Cunard continued to build paddle-steamers for their Atlantic service until as late as 1861. However, this example was constructed in 1841 by John Wood & Co. for the Eastern Steam Navigation Company.

Mahogany and pine, English, dated 1841, 63cm (36in) long

Half-block model of the merchant ship *Galaxy*

This is a simple builder's model with no deck details; its bowsprit is merely painted on to the wooden backing. Many modern replica half-block models look like this example and occasionally old wood is used for the wall panel. These replicas can sometimes be identified by carefully inspecting the paint, which often appears too bright and clean, and also the shape of the hull, which does not conform to any known vessel.

Mahogany and pine, English, late 19th century, 124cm (45in) long

Camper & Nicholson builder's half-block model of *Volador*

The combination of light and dark wood is used to represent the various waterlines, and adds to the attractiveness of this model of a 21-foot class of yacht.

Pine and mahogany, English, c.1886, 86.7 x 28.3 x 10.9cm (34¼ x 11¼ x 4¼in) (excluding backboard)

Shipbuilder's presentation model of the lifeboat *Janet Hoyle*

Lifeboat models, such as this one, were often presented to the benefactor who had funded the construction of the original vessel. This example is fitted with oars, rigging and sails, and the base is mounted with a silver plaque engraved 'Model of the Lifeboat Janet Hoyle. Stationed at Ayr, under the management of the Royal National Lifeboat Institution presented by the Institution to T. K. Hardie Esq., 1887'.

Walnut, mahogany and silver, Scottish, 1887, 53cm (21in) long

Model of the Royal Yacht *Victoria & Albert*

Models of famous ships, such as the *Victoria & Albert*, would have been made in small quantities for public display
The *Victoria & Albert* was the first British Royal Yacht to be driven by steam-power using paddle-wheels. She was laid down at Pembroke Dockyard on 9 November 1842 and built to the designs of Sir William Symonds.
Launched on 26 April 1843, she was commissioned on 1 July that year. In 1849 she carried Queen Victoria to Ireland on the occasion of her Royal visit, and was also used for Her Majesty's first Naval Review at Spithead in 1853.

Mahogany, pine and boxwood, English, mid-19th century, 144cm (56½in) long

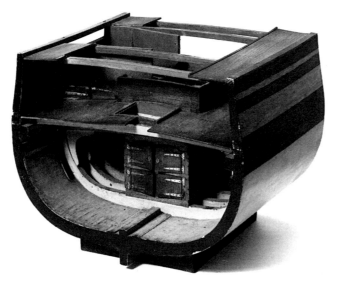

Shipbuilder's model of a ship's section

In order to show the internal construction of a full-size ship, builders occasionally produced sections of the ship's hull. This example shows the ribbing and planking of the hull and internal construction of the main-mast support and hatches.

Pine, mahogany and brass, English, mid-19th century, 35cm (13½in) wide

Shipbuilder's display model of the fishing vessel *Liraña*

To promote their business, shipbuilders sometimes produced fine-quality models of humble craft, such as fishing boats, and mounted them in attractive display cases. The *Lirana* has silver-plated fittings and well-detailed features including a linen steadying sail, navigation lights, deck winches and a superstructure with wheel-house, deck lights, stayed funnel, duck-boards and a lifeboat on chocks.

Mahogany and silver-plated metal, Scottish, late 19th century, 26 x 54.5cm (10¾ x 21½in)

Shipbuilder's display model of the dredging platform *Lagayan of Nassau*

Models of specialist craft, such as this dredger, are of interest to collectors due to their rarity. Small numbers of these vessels were made specifically for African and South American countries, where the river systems quickly silted up and dredging was a constant operation.
The *Lagayan* was built with a barge hull that could be secured to the river bed by three legs. The upper deck contained crew accommodation, ventilators and companionways, while the lower deck housed the dredging unit and its associated winch mechanism, pulleys and hose reels.

Brass, silver-plated metal, mahogany and pine, English, early 20th century, 53.5 x 96.5cm (21 x 38in)

Shipbuilder's display model of the steamship *Banshee*

Shipbuilders' models were often given to the new owner of the ship as a gift and had to depict, in every detail, the full-size version.

Brass, silver-plated metal, mahogany, satinwood and ebony, English, 1901, 150cm (59in) long

Shipbuilder's display model of the steam yacht *Venetia*

The fine lines of this type of privately owned vessel make them a favourite with collectors. During the late 19th and early 20th centuries, such pleasure-ships were built to the specifications of their wealthy aristocratic or industrialist owners to take them cruising in the North Sea or Mediterranean during the season.
Built in 1892 for Lord Ashburton, the *Venetia* was fitted with every conceivable luxury of the period and all decks were fitted with canvas canopies to protect promenaders from the sun. There were two steam launches for ferrying guests to and from ports of call.

Mahogany and gilt brass, Scottish, 1892, 171cm (67½in) long

The pond-yacht *Eigena*

The sleek lines of these model yachts followed, quite closely, those of the large 'J'-class yachts that raced at Cowes. The wooden hulls were fitted with heavy lead keels, and were sold in pine carrying cases with two or more sets of sails for different sailing conditions.

Pine and mahogany, English, early 20th century, 203 x 194cm (79 x 76in)

Bassett-Lowke model of the White Star liner R.M.S. *Titanic*

This well-detailed model of the infamous liner, *Titanic*, is finished in the White Star livery and mounted on four turned brass columns in a glazed mahogany display case. The largest ship in the world at 46,328 tons, R.M.S. *Titanic* struck an iceberg in the North Atlantic on her maiden voyage in 1912, and sank with the loss of 1,490 lives.

Mahogany and brass, English, second quarter of the 20th century, 35.5 x 188.5cm (14 x 54½in)

Shipbuilder's model of a racing yacht

In the early years of the 19th century, the designs of racing yachts were largely based on those of the revenue cutters, then the fastest vessels afloat. The rig consisted of a jib set at the end of a long bowsprit, a staysail, a gaff mainsail and upper and lower square topsails.

Such designs were broadly used until the middle of the century when, in 1851, the yacht *America* came to Cowes and proved too fast for other vessels to catch. The *America* was a schooner of 170 tons built in New York specially to race at Cowes. She came first in a race around the Isle of Wight, winning the cup presented by the Royal Yacht Squadron, known ever since as the 'America's Cup'.

Mahogany, English, mid-19th century, 88cm (34½in) long

Patent model of a ship's paddle-wheel

Models were often made and submitted, together with drawings, to the patent office for all types of inventions and ideas. This wheel has adjustable blades that offer the maximum surface area while submerged in the water and then, when out of the water, turn to present the minimum surface area, thereby reducing wind resistance.

Mahogany and brass, English, mid-19th century, 51cm (20in) wide

Presentation casket for the launching of H.M.S. *Espigle*

Caskets containing an ornately carved fruitwood chisel and mallet, were traditionally given to the dignitary who performed the launching ceremony. This example is carved from oak with stylized dolphin feet, and the inner lid inset with a watercolour of the vessel signed 'R. Rigby'.

Oak, steel, velvet and paper, English, late 19th century, 38cm (15in) wide

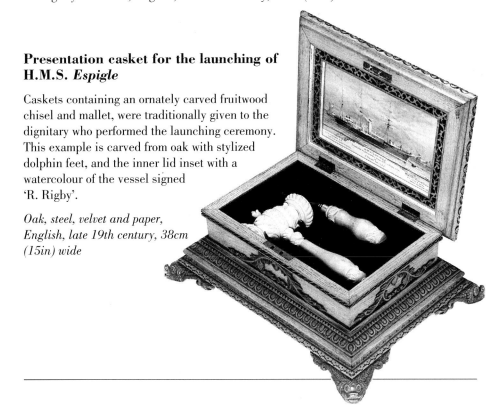

Shipbuilder's display model of a 10-gun corvette

This 1:48 scale builder's model is fitted with eleven guns on carriages and two carronades that are able to move along the deck on brass rails or traverses. The four ship's boats are mounted on davits, with one on the main deck, one each to port and starboard and one at the stern. The bows are decorated with a carved and painted female figurehead. The mahogany base has an original paper label giving the dimensions and

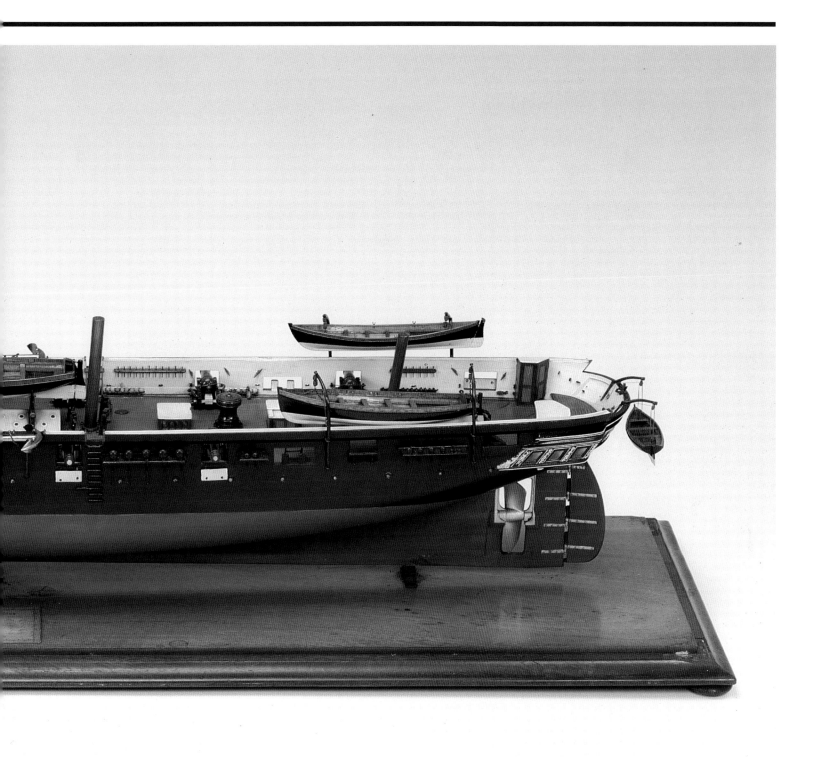

other specifications: 'Corvett of Ten Guns, Length Between Perpendiculars 157ft 6in, Length of Keel for tonnage 135ft 10in, Breadth Extreame [sic] 30ft 8in, Breadth for Tonnage 30ft 4in, Breadth Moulded 29ft 10in, Depth in Hold 15ft 10in, Burden in Tons No 679'.
Mahogany and boxwood, English, mid-19th century, 117cm (46in) long

Votive models

From the early fourteenth century, it was traditional in Europe to hang ship models in the churches of seaports and fishing communities. These were known as votive models and were made by sailors as an offering of thanks to a patron saint for having preserved the boat and its crew from the perils of the sea.

In general, the construction of such models was rather crude, with fittings, rigging and hull shapes being exaggerated in order to be seen from afar. They were often made by the ship's carpenter or another member of the crew who had little technical skill. The deck was frequently left bare since this area was obscured from the viewer's eye when the model was suspended from the roof of a church. The tradition continued into the nineteenth century, by which time the quality of the construction had increased. However, having been exposed to years of candle smoke, dampness and worm damage, the majority of such models remaining in churches are in poor condition.

Sailor-made models

From the early nineteenth century, it became quite common for sailors, and in some cases lighthouse keepers, to make ship models in their spare time. Such models varied greatly both in design and quality, many having hulls carved from a solid piece of wood, such as mahogany or pine, with string for rigging, glass beads for blocks and paper for sails. The fittings were often made of lead, which deteriorated over time, in addition to which the acid fumes emitted from wooden cases, especially oak, tended to accelerate this corrosive action. This may explain why, today, many such models appear in poor condition.

The size of these models was often limited by the sailor's cramped storage and living conditions. They fall into the following categories: ships housed in bottles, hulls mounted on bases with rigging, and waterline models set on simulated seas in cases with painted backgrounds. As the model-maker did not have access to accurate plans, the proportions of the hull, especially below the waterline, and the height of the masts tended to be inaccurate. However, the details of deck layout and rigging were often quite accurate, since this was the part of the ship with which the model-maker was most familiar. Such models have a naïve charm, making them a decorative addition to any collection.

The process by which the model-maker decorates the inside of a bottle, constructs a model with folding masts, inserts it through the neck of the bottle and then re-erects the masts and rigging, continues to fascinate collectors. Such skills have been passed down from the mid-nineteenth century to the present day, and museum shops still find them a saleable commodity.

Another type of popular decorative model, made in quite large numbers, is the 'picture model', so called because it combines the skills of the marine artist with those of the model-maker. The waterline model is mounted on a simulated sea against a painted seascape background and housed within a gilded gesso picture frame to enable hanging. Convention dictates that the vessel is almost always shown with set sails, made either from wood or metal plate. As in the case of ship portraits, a number of such models were named after relatives of the maker or the recipient of the gift, thereby precluding any positive identification of the vessel.

Sailor-made picture model of a merchant ship

This three-masted vessel, flying the Union Jack and red ensign, has painted and carved wood sails, and is mounted as a half-model on a carved and painted sea, against a sky background painted with a lighthouse, the whole within a glazed maple frame.

Pine, maple and glass, English, c.1880, 71cm (21in) wide

Sailor-made shipping diorama

The waterline model of the clipper, with paper sails and flying the red ensign and company pennants, is set on a carved and painted sea with small, out-of-scale models of a cutter, a steamboat and a paddle-steamer. The whole diorama is housed in a mahogany display case with carved ropework decoration.

Mahogany, pine and paper, English, late 19th century, 99cm (39in) long

Sailor-made picture model of the paddle-steamer *Petrel*

The waterline model of the paddle-steamer, with figures of the crew mounted on her deck, is set on a sea containing a smaller model of a steamboat, and housed in a glazed, cork-mounted frame with painted seascape background.

Cork, pine and glass, English, c.1870, 99cm (39in) wide

Sailor-made picture model of an American clipper

Flying the American flag and shipping line pennants, this half-block model is riding a stormy sea carved from wood and set against a background painted with billowing clouds and containing three other ships, within a glazed rosewood-veneered case.

Pine and rosewood, American or English, c.1880, 41 x 61cm (16 x 24in)

Sailor-made picture model of a coble

A coble is a flat-bottomed, carvel-built fishing boat used in coastal waters, particularly off Northumberland. Equipped for rowing with three sets of oars and with a mast and lugsail, one of the coble's most distinctive features is a rudder which extends about four feet below the keel. This carved and painted half-block model is set against a background painted with a harbour scene from the north-east of England.

Pine and mahogany, English, late 19th century, 38 x 61cm (15 x 24in)

Prisoner-of-war models

Some of the most enchanting models were made by Frenchmen captured by the British during the Napoleonic Wars of 1792-1815. It has been estimated that during the years 1803-14, some 122,000 captured soldiers and sailors were brought into Great Britain. Owing to a lack of prisons in which to house such a large population, these unfortunate prisoners were initially incarcerated in prison-ships known as 'hulks', so called because they had been stripped of all masts, rigging, sails, decorations and embellishments, resulting in an uncomfortable communal existence. These vessels were moored in a variety of rivers and harbours around the coast, including Sheerness, Chatham, Portsmouth, and Plymouth. The first purpose-built institution to house prisoners-of-war was completed in 1796, at Norman Cross outside Peterborough. It was designed to hold a maximum of 7,000 men and was followed in 1806 by the construction of Princetown Prison on Dartmoor, providing for a further 6,000 inmates. Whilst ordinary soldiers and sailors were strictly confined to such prisons, officers above a certain rank could choose to be placed on parole. This allowed them to be housed in private accommodation, often billetted with English families, or in prisons with the freedom to go outside the prison walls on trust. Although officers and lower

Prisoner-of-war boxwood model of the 48-gun ship-of-the-line *Glory*

The raw materials required to make *Glory*, such as copper for the hull sheath and boxwood for the body, would not have been readily available to the French prisoners within the confines of prisons, such as Norman Cross or Princetown. However, the inmates were allowed to visit local markets, where they were able to sell their wares, and thus buy provisions and materials needed for constructing models. As the original rigging was probably made from hair, which deteriorates fairly quickly, this example has been re-rigged and, during the middle of the 19th century, mounted on a mirrored base.

Boxwood, mahogany, copper and mirrored glass, French, c.1805, 51 x 71cm (20 x 28in)

**Prisoner-of-war bone model
of a 94-gun ship-of-the-line**

This standard type of prisoner model
is made from beef bones with a
pinned-and-planked hull and with a
figurehead of a warrior holding a
shield and spear. This example also
incorporates the novel feature of being
able to retract and run out the guns by
pulling the string and toggle located
at the stern. Another attractive feature
is the octagonal base, which is
painted with a stylized sea within a
leafy border.

*Bone, horn and pine, French, c.1810,
47 x 53cm (18¼ x 23in)*

ranks received a daily allowance, there was little left over to buy luxuries or to partake in the
ever-popular pursuit of gambling. No provision was made for the inmates' gainful employment,
and therefore it was not surprising that some turned their hand to producing decorative articles to
be sold at local markets. This enterprise clearly met with approval of the authorities, for a
Parliamentary report of 25 July 1800 states, 'The prisoners in all the depots in the country are at
full liberty to exercise their industry within the prisons, in manufacturing and selling articles
they may think proper . . . . and by means of this privilege some of them have been known to carry
off upon their release more than one hundred guineas each'.

These articles included straw-work sewing and toilet boxes, bone games caskets and toys,
model guillotines and, of course, ship models. It has to be remembered that the inmates were
predominantly conscripts, some of whom would have been craftsmen prior to being pressed into
the forces. It can be assumed that some of the prisoners would have been conscripted from the
French port of Dieppe which was, at the time, the centre of European trade with the Ivory Coast
and had possessed a thriving ivory carving industry long before the outbreak of the Napoleonic

Wars. Brittany, too, had a tradition of craftsmen working in jet and ivory and, as some of these artisans were captives for more than twelve years, they would have had plenty of time to instruct apprentices and pass on their expertise.

The quality of both construction and detailing suggests that many of these pieces were made collectively, with individuals combining their specialist skills in carving, turning or the working of human hair to make the rigging. Materials used were dyed straw, the left-over bones from meal-times, horn and fruitwood, the latter two of which were bartered for at the market place where such models were often sold. Wooden models normally showed much greater detail, since the medium was easier to work than bone. Many, for example, included guns which could be retracted into the decks and 'fired' by pulling chords at the stern.

It was possible for the larger and more impressive models to command prices of up to forty pounds, which was a considerable sum of money, equivalent at that time to the annual pay of a worker, and an obvious reflection of the high esteem in which these models were held by patrons. Such high prices encouraged other inmates to produce similar artefacts for sale. Unfortunately, possessing only limited skills, the finished products were models completely out of proportion and with virtually no detailing.

Models made in the prisoner-of-war style continued to be fashioned throughout the nineteenth century, right up to the present day. However, they can be easily identified as replicas, since either the construction material is inconsistent with the purported period, or the style of decoration is very different from that of the early 1800s.

Although these Napoleonic models are normally referred to as French prisoner-of-war models, there is no reason to suppose that the French were the sole nationality to make them. However, the majority of makers were certainly French, since many models show French characteristics of style and decoration, French names and flags, and French hall-marks in the hull design and rigging. According to contemporary prison registers, there were also prisoners from Italy, Switzerland, Spain, Holland and the Americas. In fact, the National Maritime Museum at Greenwich has a World War I model of the *Scharnhorst*, the German armoured cruiser built in 1906, which took part in the Battle of the Falklands in 1914. The model was made by German prisoners-of-war aboard H.M.S. *Invincible*, following the battle. There is only one known example of a model being made by a British prisoner-of-war in France, and that is a rather crude fifty-two-gun warship now housed in Le Musée d'Art et d'Histoire in Geneva.

Dieppe ivory models

From the 1830s onwards, many ship models were produced in the workshops of Dieppe, and although often described as prisoner-of-war models, they were completely different both in construction and style. Their hulls were always carved from a single, solid piece of ivory, rather than bone, the rigging and sails were made from ivory strands and shavings, and there were normally some miniature figures placed on the deck. In general, the models were between three and five inches long and normally protected by a glazed case. They have a very delicate quality and charm which is, at best, an accolade to the art of the ivory carver.

Prisoner-of-war boxwood model of H.M.S. *Victory*

This model of the *Victory* was made as a memorial to Admiral Lord Nelson and carries a model of Nelson's tomb on the main deck, adorned with a coat of arms, flags, banners and trophies of war. The sides of the tomb are carved in relief with panels depicting naval engagements. Nelson was certainly one of the most popular of British heroes, and much commemorative ware was produced at the time of his death. His impressive state funeral was held on 8 January 1806 and his body, contained within a coffin made from the wood of the main-mast of *L'Orient*, was laid to rest in St Paul's Cathedral.

Boxwood, French, c.1806, 46cm (18in) long

Prisoner-of-war boxwood model of a 94-gun ship-of-the-line

This small, finely detailed boxwood model is mounted on a base inlaid with bone and horn. The contemporary carrying case would also have been made by prisoners from wood applied with coloured straw laid in an intricate geometric pattern. To enable the owner to inspect the far side of the model, three mirrored glass panels have been mounted on the inside back surface. To add to the overall dramatic effect, the maker has installed pink silk curtains on either side of the case.

Boxwood, bone and horn, French, c.1810, the model 28 x 18cm (9½ x 7in)

Prisoner-of-war miniature boxwood model of a ship-of-the-line

More a work of miniature art than a model, this boxwood example is only two inches high and includes all the detailing and features of much larger models.

The sails and rigging are carved from wood, and the deck is fitted with details so small that a glass is needed to see them properly. The model has a carved figurehead, guns on carriages, capstan, bell canopy, ship's boats and belaying rails. It is mounted on a tiered boxwood stand with six classical statues, set beneath a glass dome.

Boxwood and glass, French, early 19th century, ship model 5 x 7.5cm (2 x 3in); 12 x 12.5cm (4¾ x 5in) overall

Boxwood and ivory miniature display of four ship models

This lavish miniature depicts two ivory models of the ships-of-the-line, *La Qualiaque* and *Le Stately*, each with transparent horn sails and carved and painted ivory figureheads. Also on the stand are models of a brigantine and a cutter. All four models are mounted on a galleried boxwood stand decorated with six Classical figures, and the whole positioned under a canopy raised on four ivory columns, applied overall with carved acanthus leaf decoration and both the British and Admiral Nelson's coats of arms.

Boxwood and ivory, French, early 19th century, 12.8 x 15 x 11cm (5 x 6 x 4¼in)

Prisoner-of-war bone model of a 102-gun ship-of-the-line

This attractive model, with a carved bone warrior figurehead and red-painted gun ports, is unusual in that it possesses contemporary paper sails. The deck is fitted with a capstan, a stove pipe above the gallery, a ship's bell under a canopy, and deck skylights.

Bone and paper, French, c.1800, 32 x 34cm (12⅓ x 13½in)

Dieppe ivory model of a frigate

The ivory carving industry in Dieppe produced a wide range of decorative wares during the 19th century, including some delightful ivory ship models. These can be distinguished from the prisoner-of-war models by their all-ivory construction, their carved ivory sails and rigging, and a delicacy of handling often lacking in other models.

Ivory and ebonized wood, French, c.1830, 18cm (7in) high

Dieppe miniature ship portrait panel

This unusual oval, carved ivory panel shows the crew members of a frigate working on deck and in the rigging, together with tiny details such as ratlines, gun ports, lanterns and cannons. The ship is set on a choppy sea made from strands of ivory, with a fishing smack in the foreground and other square-rigged vessels in the distance.

Ivory, French, mid-19th century, 8.5 x 7.3cm (3⅜ x 2⅞in)

Modern models made by amateurs

There is an ever-growing interest in the design and construction of historic and contemporary ships and boats by the amateur model-maker. The best modern models compare favourably with some exceptionally fine eighteenth- and nineteenth-century examples now housed in museum collections. Today, there are many specialist magazines available to the enthusiast, providing information on technique, design and tools, in addition to which many marine museums sell copies of the plans of historic ships, from which the model-maker can produce a miniature replica. The best examples reflect not only the maker's understanding of the complex construction of the plank-on-frame hull, but also the fine quality of their carving of deck details and their comprehension of the intricacies of standing-and-running rigging. Many of these scratch-built models can take thousands of hours to design and construct. However, for the less ambitious there are numerous kits readily available with pre-made constituents.

Such renewal of interest in the craft of boat and ship model building will ensure that future generations have a comprehensive, three-dimensional record of today's sea-going vessels.

Modern model of the sixth-rate H.M.S. *Liverpool*

Made by John Taylor in the style of a Dockyard model, the planking has been removed to show the internal construction of the ship. This finely detailed model includes a carved and painted rampant lion figurehead, and a deck with ship's wheel, fire buckets, belaying rails and pins, stove pipe and anchors.

Boxwood, English, modern, 89cm (35in) long

Navigational Instruments

THE TWO principal factors to be determined by the navigator are the plotting of a course between two known points and the ship's position at any time.

As long as a ship sailed along the coast, determining its position was not too difficult; the pilot merely had to supplement his local knowledge with the use of a magnetic compass, a sand-glass and a lead and line to take soundings. However, out of sight of land the navigator had to determine the two coordinates of latitude and longitude. During the sixteenth and seventeenth centuries the navigator had two options: to keep an account of the ship's speed and changes of direction since leaving port, or the last known sighting of land, this being known as 'dead reckoning'; or alternatively, to make use of the known positions of the sun, moon and stars relative to the ship's position.

Direction finding and recording instruments

The compass

The compass is the navigational instrument by which a ship may be steered on a pre-selected course, and by which bearings of visible objects may be taken to fix a ship's position on a sea chart. There are two types: the magnetic compass, indicating the magnetic north pole, and the gyro compass, indicating the true north.

The early history of the magnetic compass is uncertain, although the magnetized needle was certainly in use in Europe by the twelfth century. The needle was magnetized by stroking it with a naturally occurring, soft magnetic iron ore, known as a lodestone. It was then either floated in a bowl of water with the needle mounted on a straw or sliver of wood, or set on a pivot, and revolved until it aligned in the direction of magnetic north.

By the beginning of the fourteenth century the magnetized needle had been placed under a compass card and both enclosed within a box. However, it was not until the fifteenth century that the north European tradition of the thirty-two point compass rose became universal. During this time it became apparent that the needle was not pointing to true north, and compass makers subsequently made allowances for this by offsetting the needle (mounted below the card) by a few degrees. It also became clear that the magnetic variation was different, both in terms of magnitude and direction, in different parts of the world, and the practice, therefore, of making allowances in the construction of compasses gradually became accepted by the end of the seventeenth century.

To offer protection to the compass, and to allow for the pitch and roll of the ship, the compass card was pivoted in a brass drum-shaped bowl and set within two concentric metal rings, known as gimbals. These were set on knife-edges at opposing quadrants, thus allowing the compass to remain level. By the beginning of the nineteenth century the compass was mounted beneath a brass domed cover, known as a binnacle, which had an observation window and a light for night viewing.

Föhr-type octant

This all-brass instrument has an A-shaped frame, ornately engraved with acanthus leaves, and a stretcher in the form of a flower seller. The 0-90 degree scale allows readings to within one degree, and the index arm has a diagonal scale permitting readings to the nearest five minutes. The instrument comes complete with sighting vane, horizon glass and two coloured filters. This attractive type of instrument was made by Jan Cornelisz who worked on the German Frisian island of Föhr.

Brass, German, c.1760, 21.5cm (8½in) radius

Hanging tell-tale ship's compass

The printed compass card is pivoted and set within a gilt-metal, crown-shaped case with a suspension loop above. The card is inscribed 'Iver Jensen Borger Kiobenhaven'.
This ornate type of compass was hung from the deck beams in a cabin so that, while away from the bridge, the officers would know the ship's direction.

Card, glass and gilt metal, Danish, late 18th or early 19th century, 20cm (8in) high

Small lodestone in a fish-skin case

This pocket example was probably made for a wealthy person, since the mounts are of silver and it is housed in a fitted pocket-case. The two small iron poles are just visible below the lower silver mount, and the instrument was designed to be suspended by the shaped loop at the top.

Iron, silver, card and fish-skin, English, second half of the 18th century, 5cm (2in) high

Keen's patent porcelain cabin compass bowl

The ceramic bowl is decorated with a cobalt-blue band and applied with transfer decoration, together with a coat of arms on the inside wall. The pivoted compass card is signed 'J. Hughes, Queen St., Ratcliff London', and is mounted with two strips of steel bar magnets. The magnets are pivoted half-way along their length and thus should remain horizontal whilst the ship moves. The compass card is also set within small gimbals to ensure that it, too, remains horizontal at all times.
A Joseph Hughes is recorded as having worked at Queen Street from 1822 to 1846.

Ceramic, steel, card and glass, English, c.1830, 26.5cm (10½in) diameter

Henry Hughes & Son Pelorus dial

The Pelorus was used for taking the magnetic bearing of objects obscured from the standard compass. It consisted of a brass plate engraved with compass points, but with no magnets, and sights which were pivoted about the centre. The whole was set inside gimbals and mounted in a wooden case, and a set of instructions pasted to the inside of the lid. The term, 'Pelorus', is derived from the name of Hannibal's pilot, who assisted him in getting his troops across Europe and who kept him in touch with Carthage by sea.

Brass and mahogany, English, late 19th century, in case 30.5cm (12in) wide

Kelvin White binnacle compass

The compass ring floats in a liquid beneath the semi-spherical glass cover, and the whole is mounted in gimbals beneath the binnacle with six glass windows on a circular brass base. The purpose of a binnacle was both to protect the compass from the elements and to provide a means of illuminating it at night. In older ships the binnacle also provided stowage for the traverse board, the log line reel and the sand-glass.

Brass, glass and card, English, late 19th century, 33cm (13in) high

The introduction of iron and steel in ship construction during the early nineteenth century, caused considerable deviation of the compass needle and therefore various methods of neutralizing this effect were developed. These included mounting pieces of magnetic and non-magnetic iron in the vicinity of the compass, often as part of the binnacle itself.

Dry card compasses were made in considerable numbers during the eighteenth and nineteenth centuries, and one of the more unusual types was the so-called tell-tale. This contained a compass card with reversed east and west points, since it was designed to be suspended upside down above the captain's bunk, allowing him to follow the ship's direction while resting. Often mounted in gimbals, these compasses, though normally of plain construction, sometimes incorporated elaborate crown-shaped decoration in brass above the compass bowl.

During the eighteenth century the floating compass card was housed in a brass bowl, filled with a clear liquid such as spirits of wine, and the magnets, being more permanent by this time, did not need refreshing with a lodestone.

The dry card compass was reintroduced by Sir William Thomson, later Lord Kelvin, in 1876 and was used by merchant navies well into this century. Kelvin's design incorporated a compass card constructed from very light paper, with an aluminium ring running round the circumference and the whole suspended from a jewelled pivot by silk thread.

The gyroscopic compass was first introduced in 1908 by the German engineer, Anschutz. It worked on the principle of the compass card being mounted within an electrically driven spinning wheel, and was designed to point to the true north pole rather than the magnetic pole.

The traverse board

The traverse board was known to be in existence by the sixteenth century and was still being used by Baltic navigators in the nineteenth century. The ship's master could record the bearings indicated by the compass on a wooden board by means of pegs, which could be inserted in holes arranged in eight radiating lines. At the end of each half-hour, one of the eight pegs was inserted into the hole representing the compass bearing along which the ship had run during that period. At the end of the watch, the mean course was calculated from the position of the pegs.

Sand-glasses

The sand-, or watch-glass was normally constructed to run for a period of half an hour, although one- and four-hour glasses also existed. They all consisted of two joined, shaped glass bulbs filled with iron filings, marble dust or powdered egg shell, and set within a framework of wood, ivory or metal. The two bulbs were normally bound together using twine and wax, and it was not until the end of the eighteenth century that the technique was perfected for blowing a single waisted glass vessel.

The seaman's day was divided into four-hour watches. Thus, there were six watches in a day, each watch being split into eight bells. The more usual glass was the half-hour glass, and this was turned by the ship's boy who, at the same time, rang a bell to mark the event. After eight bells the watch was changed and the series of eight bells started again, beginning at noon. For greater accuracy, several glasses were sometimes built into one casing, either to run for the same length of time and a mean reading taken, or alternatively running for a quarter-, half-, three-quarters and one hour respectively.

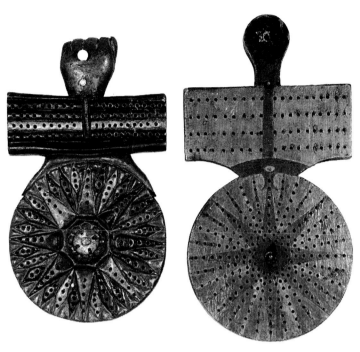

Two carved and painted wood traverse boards

The circular dials are carved with thirty-two points of the compass and contain a series of holes. By inserting pegs in the holes to represent compass readings taken over a given period, the direction sailed by the vessel can be determined. The rectangular boards above, again containing a series of holes, record the log speed.

Carved and painted wood, probably Italian, 17th century, 32cm (12½in) long (left); carved and painted wood, German or English, 19th century, 37cm (14½in) long (right)

Set of four sand-glasses

This set measures the quarter-, half-, three-quarter and one hour respectively. All are mounted in a brass frame with a pierced gallery border.

Glass, brass, wax, twine and sand, French, late 18th century, 21.5cm (8½in) wide

Sand-glass or hour-glass

Before the development of reliable clocks, sand-glasses were one means of measuring the passage of time on board ship. The basic sand-glass consisted of two glass bulbs connected by a narrow neck, through which sand passed within a given interval of time. When the sand had completely run through, the glass was turned the other way up and the process repeated. Sand-glasses were made for maritime use in four sizes: half-minute, half-hour, hour and four-hour.

This example of a large hour-glass is unusual in that one of the bulbs is blown in three-tear form, probably to show the passage of the quarter hours. The two glass bulbs are connected by wax and twine and mounted in a brass frame.

Glass, brass, wax, twine and sand, French, late 18th century, 30.5cm (12in) high

NAUTICAL ANTIQUES & COLLECTABLES

The log

The 'log' was first described in William Bourne's *Regiment for the Sea*, written in 1574, as being a piece of shaped wood with a weight attached at one end in order that it should float upright in the water. The log was attached by three short pieces of rope to the so-called 'log line' and the log was cast astern of the vessel. The log line was knotted at regular intervals and the number of knots played out during a period of half a minute, again timed by a log glass, was counted. This operation provides the origin of the expression for describing the speed of a ship in 'knots'.

Although a number of mechanical logs were patented during the eighteenth century, examples exist from as far back as the sixteenth century. However, the first reliable log was not developed until 1802, when Edward Massey invented a spinning brass rotor which recorded the distance travelled by a ship on a series of dials, and these could then be read when the log was retrieved from the sea. A modification of this was the taff-rail log, introduced in the late 1840s, in which the recording device was attached to the 'taff', or stern rail, of the ship and connected to the rotor by means of a length of rope. Such logs were made in considerable quantities and are still quite easy to find today in their original boxes.

Another means of determining speed was by using the 'Dutchman's log', popular with seafarers from the Netherlands in the seventeenth and eighteenth centuries. A float was thrown from the bow of the ship and subsequently timed between two fixed points on the ship's side. The speed of the ship could then be determined by using conversion tables, which were sometimes engraved on objects such as oblong brass tobacco boxes.

Calculating longitude through astronomy

The theory of determining longitude at sea through astronomical observation was understood by the sixteenth century. However, the technology necessary to take such readings did not become available until the eighteenth century. It consisted of using the measurement of angular distance of the moon in relation to certain prominent stars, together with a set of standard tables. Known as the 'lunar distance' method, the system was used in conjunction with a cross-staff, and later the sextant or the reflecting circle.

The reflecting circle

The 'lunar distance' theory of determining longitude was initially the work of the German astronomer, Johann Tobias Mayer (1723-62), whose lunar tables were published in *The British Mariner's Guide* of 1763 by the Cambridge astronomer, Nevil Maskelyne (1732-1811). Meyer also designed an instrument based on the same principle as the sextant, but with a full circle divided into 720 degrees. The sighting telescope and horizon mirror could be moved to any position on the circle. These were then clamped and the index arm moved around the circle until the two objects being measured effected an apparent conjunction. The angle to be measured was the difference between the two readings. However, the operation had to be repeated a number of times and a mean reading taken, hence the instrument is sometimes known as a 'repeating circle'.

Ship's automatic log register

Mounted on a shaped mahogany backboard, the clock has an eight-day movement and a paper dial inscribed 'The Nautical Instrument Co. Stockholm', together with a brass dial with a 1-100 scale and a brass bell above. The register would have recorded the speed of a ship at specific times during the day.

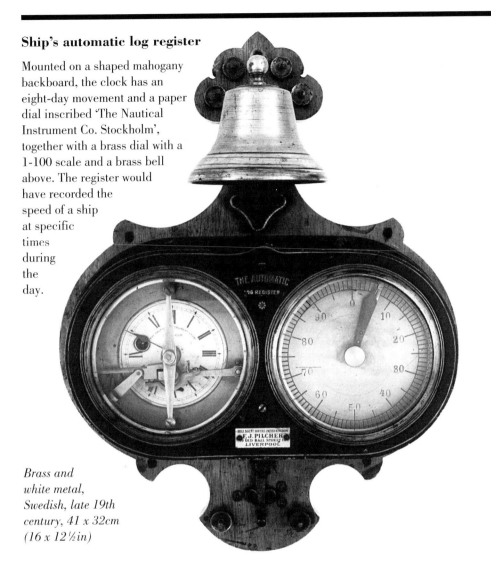

Brass and white metal, Swedish, late 19th century, 41 x 32cm (16 x 12½in)

Set of four sand-glasses

The carved and gilt-painted wooden frame, housing the four glass ampoules, has an axle attached to the back. Originally, this would have allowed the instrument to be mounted next to the seaman on watch and, when all the sand had run through, for it to be swivelled up-side-down and the process repeated. This arrangement would have been safer than having the sand-glass loose on deck.

Wood, glass and sand, German, early 18th century, 29 x 27 x 9cm (11½ x 10¾ x 3½in)

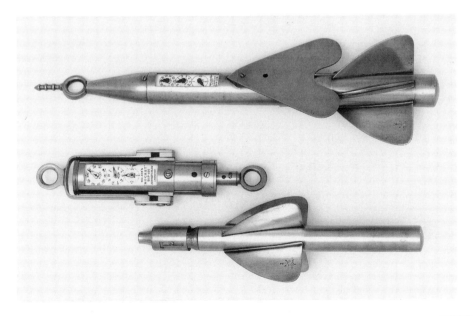

Two Walker's ships' logs

The Walker's 'Rocket' log (bottom) comprises a cylindrical brass casing containing a white enamel dial. One end is attached to the taff-rail at the stern of the ship and the eye at the other end is attached to the spinner, via a length of rope.

The 'Harpoon' log (top) does not need a taff-rail dial, as this is incorporated within the structure of the spinner.

Brass and enamel, English, late 19th century, the larger 53cm (21in) long

Brass tobacco box with engraved log and perpetual calendar

This kind of tobacco box was devised by a Swedish mariner, Pieter Holm, who established a navigation school in Antwerp during the middle of the 18th century.

The top of the box is engraved with a perpetual almanac and lunar calendar, flanked by portraits of Julius Caesar and Pope Gregory XIII. Engraved on the base is a table for calculating the speed of a ship against the time taken for a piece of wood to pass between two marked points on a ship's side.

Brass, Dutch, c.1760, 15cm (6in) long

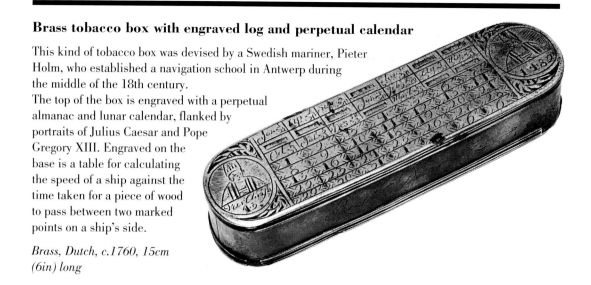

James Allen reflecting circle

The reflecting circle worked on the same principle as the sextant, but with a greater degree of accuracy. Both the sighting telescope and horizon mirror could be moved to any position on the circle and clamped. The index arm was then turned to effect an apparent conjunction of the two objects being measured. This process was repeated a number of times and an average reading taken.

This example has a brass frame with an inset silver degree circle, three index arms with silver vernier scales, two sets of coloured filters and a telescope.

Brass, silver and mahogany, English, early 19th century, 25.5cm (10in) diameter

The most common type of English reflecting circle appeared in the late eighteenth century, and followed Edward Troughton's fixed telescope design. The French physicist, Jean-Charles Borda (1733-99), invented an improved design for the repeating circle. It was produced in considerable numbers, both in France, by makers such as Lenoir, Gambey and Secretan, and in England by Troughton, Dollond and James Allen.

Chronometers

The easiest and most accurate method of finding the longitude at sea was by comparing the time on an accurate clock, known as a chronometer, set to the time at the ship's home port, with that of a measurement of the local time at the ship's position, found by sighting the sun at noon or the stars at night.

The problem was to produce a timepiece whose average rate was not affected by that of the ship, or by changes in temperature. In 1714, the Admiralty laid down strict guidelines for the accuracy of such a clock, and offered a substantial prize of £20,000 to the clockmaker who could produce such a movement. The prize was awarded to the Yorkshire clockmaker, John Harrison (1693-1776), who, in 1735, produced a marine chronometer of quite brilliant conception. The instrument, now housed in the Royal Observatory, Greenwich, stands over 40 cm high, and contains a movement regulated by the counteracting motions of two bar balances, pivoted centrally and controlled by four helical balance springs. It also incorporated Harrison's 'grasshopper' escapement and method of maintaining power, the whole machine being housed in gimbals within a spring-mounted frame.

Harrison made two more large clocks in 1737 and 1757, and finally, in 1759, a fourth, in the form of a large silver-cased pocket watch which, after successful trials on two voyages to the West Indies, eventually won the Board's prize. Although ingenious, Harrison's invention did not lead directly to the common chronometer of the nineteenth and twentieth centuries. It was the Frenchman, Pierre Le Roy, who devised new techniques in constructing the balance wheel which, with modification, formed the basis of the successful working chronometer used in the late eighteenth and early nineteenth centuries. By 1820, two firms, John Arnold and Thomas Earnshaw, had jointly perfected the modern form of chronometer movement, producing over 2,000 of such chronometers for both the Royal and Merchant Navies.

Early chronometers were sometimes mounted in brass gimbals, within eight-sided mahogany cases with glazed tops. By the early nineteenth century these had been replaced by brass bound, square section mahogany cases with double-hinged top and side carrying handles. The firms of Arnold, Dent, Frodsham, Thomas Mercer and Victor Kullberg were amongst the leading makers of such chronometers in nineteenth-century England, while in France, where there were considerably fewer makers, the trade was dominated by Le Roy and Berthoud.

Another form of navigational timepiece was the 'chronometer watch', which had some of the characteristics of the chronometer, including a chronometer compensation balance and spring detent. The ship's chronometer was not normally moved from its fixed position on board ship, and therefore the chronometer watch was used to 'carry time' from the chronometer to wherever it was needed on the ship for navigational purposes. Another variant, known as the 'deck watch', performed a similar function, but the movement was not of the same quality as that of a chronometer, as it incorporated only a lever escapement.

Noon-day gun or cannon dial

Large examples of such instruments were used in ports and military camps to signal noon, whereupon watches and clocks could be adjusted. Smaller examples, such as the present one, would have been used in private gardens, although they all worked on the same principle.

The circular marble base is engraved with an hour scale and mounted with a gnomon, a small cannon and two brackets supporting a burning lens. If the instrument is properly orientated, and the lens set to the correct solar declination, then at noon, assuming the sun is shining, the burning beam will ignite the powder and fire the gun.

Marble, bronze, brass and glass, English, c.1880, 30.5cm (12in) diameter

Edward John Dent's patent dipleidoscope

E. J. Dent, the respected chronometer maker, patented the dipleidoscope for noting the meridian passage of the sun. The instrument consisted of a right-angled prism with two silvered sides. The meridian transit was noted when the two images of the sun coincided and, when properly levelled and orientated, the instrument could determine the correct time to within seconds. Such instruments were important for checking the accuracy of chronometers.

Brass, glass and silvered metal, English, mid-19th century, 10cm (4in) square

Perpetual calendar

The pocket disk instrument shows, on one face, the day of the week together with an adjustable wheel with the date and, on the other, two slots showing sunrise and sunset times and lengths of the day and night according to the date. This example is decorated with an engraving of shipping off Amsterdam.

Brass, Dutch, late 18th century, 5cm (2in) diameter

Two one-day marine chronometers

A John Arnold one-day marine chronometer (left) with a silvered metal face, inscribed 'Arnold London No 492 One Day', and a subsidiary seconds dial. The whole mounted in brass gimbals within a mahogany double-hinged case.
Brass, steel and mahogany, English, c.1810, bezel 9cm (3½in) diameter

A Molyneux & Sons small one-day marine chronometer (right). The mahogany case, with brass strengtheners, is unusual since it has an angled glass window at the front through which the face could be viewed, unlike the more common double-hinged case with flat window.
Brass, mahogany and steel, English, c.1830, bezel 7cm (2¾in) diameter

Boxwood nocturnal

The nocturnal is a hand-held instrument that gives a rough indication of time during the hours of darkness. The rotating dial is set to the correct date and the nocturnal is then held upright by the shaped handle. The pole star is viewed through the central rivet and the large pointer is turned so as to be in line with the Guards of the Bear. The time is then indicated on the hour scale where it is cut by the pointer.

Boxwood and brass, English, mid-18th century, 23 cm (9in) high

Henry Appleton two-day marine chronometer

The enamel dial contains an hour scale, with two subsidiary dials for seconds, and an up-and-down dial indicating the number of hours remaining until the movement requires rewinding. The instrument can be locked into a fixed position, while being carried, by engaging the lever and screw located on the right-hand side of the box. This example has the tester's certificate of accuracy still pasted to the inside of the lid. The mahogany case is fitted with brass carrying handles and strengtheners.

Brass, glass, steel and mahogany, English, c.1840, bezel 10cm.(4in) diameter

J. R. Arnold eight-day marine chronometer

The movement is based on John Arnold's original marine chronometer, which was later finished by
J. R. Arnold as an eight-day chronometer with an Arnold's spring detent escapement. Signed 'John R. Arnold
London Invt. et Fecit No 220'; the inside of the great wheel is signed 'W. F. Rattray finished 1804'. Mounted
in a brass box within gimbals, its mahogany case has brass carrying handles at the sides and is inset at the
front with a numbered roundel.

Brass, steel, enamel, mahogany and glass, English, 1804, bezel 14.5cm (5¾in) diameter

Instruments for the determination of latitude

It was the Portuguese, and later the Spanish, who, in their desire to create an empire during the fifteenth and sixteenth centuries, developed new techniques of instrumental navigation.

The quadrant

The simplest way to measure terrestrial latitude was by calculating the altitude of the Pole Star (Polaris), this being determined by using a portable version of the astronomer's quadrant. Constructed either in wood or metal, the quarter circle was graduated in degrees along its curved edge. Two sights were mounted along one of the straight edges and a plumb-line fixed at the apex. Altitudes were recorded by fixing the star through the sights and taking a reading from the degree scale. Unfortunately, this instrument proved impractical for use at sea, due to the movement of the ship. However, the introduction of the mariner's astrolabe in the late fifteenth century rectified some of these deficiencies.

Mariner's astrolabe

The mariner's astrolabe was, perhaps, a less sophisticated adaptation of the earlier astronomer's planispheric astrolabe, since it had only a degree scale and sighting rule, or alidade. It was made out of thick calibre brass, with a weighted base to reduce movement, and cut-out sections in the body to minimize wind resistance. The astrolabe was used to measure the altitude of the sun near the meridian. The devise was suspended by a ring, mounted at the top of the instrument; the alidade was turned until the beam of sunlight shining through the hole in the upper vane corresponded with the hole in the lower vane. The sun's altitude was then read on the degree scale. Today, more mariner's astrolabes are appearing on the market, as increasingly sophisticated methods of detection are used to recover artefacts from the seabed.

The cross-staff and the back-staff

The cross-staff was another instrument used by navigators in the sixteenth and seventeenth centuries to determine the angular elevation of a star, or the sun above the horizon, and hence to calculate the latitude of a ship. Made of wood, and sometimes ivory, the central square section rod, calibrated on all four faces, had three or four cross pieces, or 'transoms', of graduated length, each capable of moving up and down the central rod. To take a sighting, the operator would point the staff at the sun and move the transom until the lower edge touched the horizon and the top edge touched the sun. The solar altitude could then be read from the appropriate scale, the only disadvantage being that the operator had to look directly into the sun and had to spread his angle of vision.

These problems were overcome, however, by the introduction of the back-staff, a description of which can be found in John Davis's book, *The Seaman's Secrets*, written around 1585. The ebony or rosewood instrument was constructed with two boxwood calibrated arcs, and carried a moveable shadow vane and pin-hole sight. It measured the solar altitude using the sun's shadow

Mariner's astrolabe

Typical of an instrument that has spent a considerable period of time on the sea bed, this astrolabe has lost all its decoration and the scale has been worn away by the sand and sea. Originally, there would have been a suspension loop at the top from which the operator would have held the instrument while taking a sight of the sun using the alidade.

This instrument is very similar in style to that which was issued to Dutch East India Company navigators during the 17th century.

Brass, Dutch, c.1630-50, 25.5cm (10in) diameter

rather than direct sunlight, with the user sighting the horizon with his back to the sun. Back-staffs were made in considerable numbers until the middle of the eighteenth century, when they were superseded by the octant.

The octant and sextant

John Hadley published his designs for the octant in the *Philosophical Transactions of the Royal Society* in 1731. The radical departure in design from previous instruments was the introduction of a mirror, mounted over the pivot of a radial arm and which moved over a 90 degree arc. The horizon was viewed through a pin-hole sight at a rectangular half-silvered horizon glass and the radial arm was moved until the sun, sighted through the mirror half of the glass, was brought down to touch the horizon. The angle of elevation could then be read from the scale, using the vernier for readings of less than one degree.

The name, octant, derives from the fact that, although the scale can be read from 0 to 90 degrees, it actually only occupies an eighth of a circle, due to the use of the mirror. Eighteenth-century examples measure between 14 and 24 inches in radius and are constructed in mahogany with diagonal scales engraved in either ivory or boxwood. Those made after 1800 tend to have ebony frames of 12 inches radius or less, with ivory scales. They are fitted with telescopes rather than pin-hole sights and have index arms made of brass rather than wood. In addition to the marked improvement in the accuracy of measuring the altitude of a star by an octant rather than a backstaff, the coincidence of the star and the horizon was not affected by the motion of the ship.

The vernier scale was commonly used from around 1770 onwards, although the diagonal scale was still used on some cheaper instruments after this date. Until about 1780, it was more common for the zero to be placed centrally on the vernier; on later examples, however, the zero is to be found located on the right hand side. A clamping screw was fitted to the underside of the vernier to ensure that the reading could be fixed while sighting took place, and for the more expensive instruments, a tangent screw was installed to make final adjustments to the reading. The majority of eighteenth-century octants were fitted with a second pin-hole sight and horizon glass, mounted on opposing sides of the frame. Called the 'back-sight' and 'back horizon glass', they were intended to be used for measuring angles greater than 90 degrees.

The sextant was developed from the octant, and the name refers to the actual arc of the frame, which occupies a sixth of a circle, and not to the actual arc that can be measured. The need for an instrument to measure angles of up to 120 degrees arose from the necessity to make lunar observations for the determination of longitude. Although the chronometer eventually superseded this ancient method, the sextant was retained as the additional scale made it useful for reading horizontal angles and, furthermore, its all-metal construction made it more accurate than the wooden octant.

From 1800 onwards sextants were made in large numbers, with a variety of brass frames being constructed in lattice, triple circles and even bell shapes. The scales were either of silver, platinum or gold and the instrument was sold in a wooden carrying case with up to three alternative telescopes. A certificate detailing the date of the last check on the accuracy of the instrument was usually tacked to the inside of the lid. Other variations in the construction of the sextant frame included the bridge-frame and double-framed sextants, both of which were produced in limited numbers and so command greater value today.

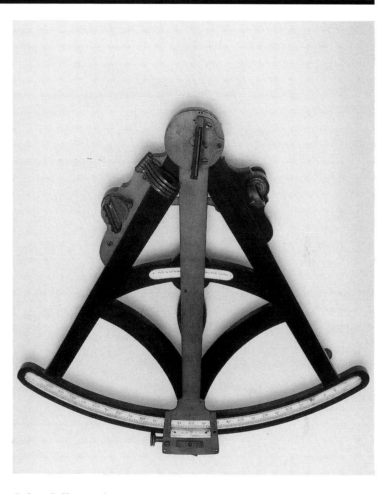

John Crichton octant

This is an example of a standard type of octant with an ebony frame and peep-hole eyepiece. Peep-holes were replaced by telescopes on later octants and on almost all sextants. The turned ivory finial visible above the maker's plaque is, in fact, the top of a lead pencil. This was used by the navigator to note his readings on a small ivory plate set into the back of the instrument.

Ebony, ivory and brass, English, c.1830, 30.5cm (12in) radius

John Gilbert ebony sextant

This instrument incorporates an ebony frame with a brass index arm, ivory scales and a maker's plaque. It is unusual to find a sextant with a wooden frame instead of brass. The name, 'sextant', derives from the fact that the scale arc occupies a sixth of a circle, while that of an octant occupies an eighth of a circle.

Ebony, ivory and brass, English, late 18th century, 33.5cm (13¼in) radius

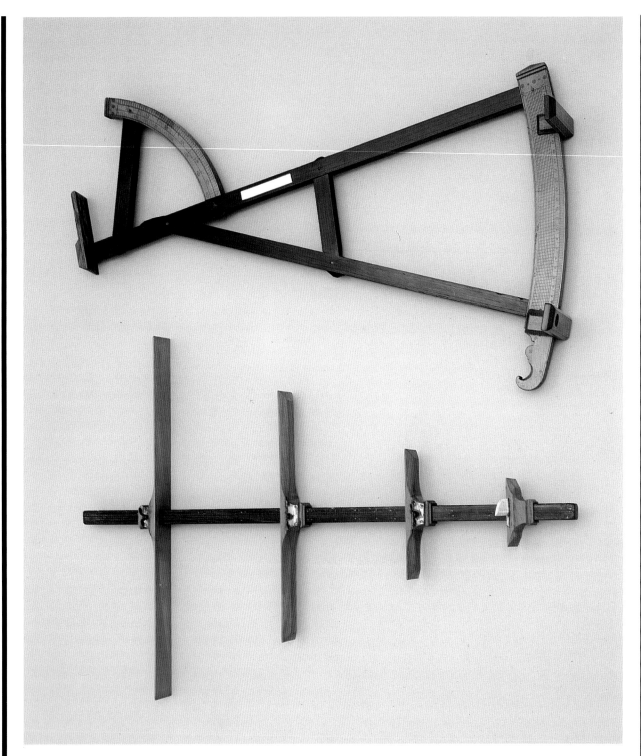

Back-staff and cross-staff

The lignum vitae and boxwood back-staff (top) has a sight vane arc numbered from 1 to 25 degrees along the outer edge, and from 65 to 90 degrees along the inner edge. The shadow arc is numbered from 0 to 62 degrees and both boxwood arcs are stamped with Tudor rose decoration.

Lignum vitae and boxwood, English, third quarter of the 18th century, 64cm (25in) long

The cross-staff (bottom) is stamped with initials 'J V K' and the date 1765, which indicates that the instrument was made by Johannes van Keulin. The transoms are later reproductions.

Lignum vitae, Dutch, dated 1765, 66cm (26in) long

John Bird mahogany and brass quadrant

This large and impressive instrument incorporates an unusual adjustment to the back horizon glass, by means of a screw and a brass strut mounted across the frame. The arc is signed 'J Bird London', and the cross strut 'Dollond London'. A patent for the accurate adjustment of the back horizon glass was taken out by Peter Dollond on 22 May 1772.

John Bird had a workshop at the Sea Quadrant, in Court Gardens on the Strand, and made several instruments for the Royal Observatory, Greenwich, as well as for other international observatories.

Mahogany and brass, English, c.1775, 50cm (20in) radius

Cased Dollond sextant

This standard sextant has a lattice frame, silver scale and a vernier with a magnifier to assist scale readings. The mahogany carrying case contains two telescopes stowed below the sextant housing.

Brass, silver and mahogany, English, early 19th century, 15cm (6in) radius

Bridge-framed sextant

A distinctive type of sextant frame was the so-called bridge-frame, which was used throughout the first half of the 19th century as a means of ensuring a very rigid instrument structure. It consisted of a series of braces mounted above the apex of the A-frame.

Brass, silver and mahogany, English, second quarter of the 19th century, 18cm (7in) radius

Charts, globes and associated instruments

Early navigators relied upon the rutter and the almanac to steer their ship through local waters. The 'rutter' was an early book of sailing directions, containing illustrations of ports and stretches of coastline viewed from the sea, the name of which derived from the French *routier* and the Portuguese *roteiro*, denoting a 'route'. In 1483, a French navigator, Pierre Garcie, wrote his *Le Grand Routier et Pilotage* describing the west coast of France. This is the earliest record of such a book. It was later translated into English, and appeared in 1521 with woodcut illustrations. It contained information about local tides and general advice to the navigator, including entries into harbours and positions of the sun, moon and stars at various times of the year. An English seaman's notebook was also referred to as a rutter. It was normally handed down from father to son, and contained records of local voyages, courses and anchorages.

Seamen's almanacs were in general circulation by the end of the fifteenth century and were either printed in broadsheet, so that they could be tacked to the cabin wall, or alternatively they were printed in small pocket-book format. They contained a wide range of information relating to navigation, weather forecasting and astronomical calendars. By the seventeenth century these almanacs had been expanded to appeal to a wider public and thus, in addition to useful information for the seafarer such as tide tables, time determination by moon phase, and high water calculations, they also listed astrological forecasts, ecclesiastical calendars and holidays.

Simple charts had been drawn by cartographers for navigators as early the first century A.D. However, it was not until 1569 that the cartographer, Gerhard Mercator (1512-94), produced a map of the globe which was to solve the navigator's problem of steering ocean courses. Mercator's map, covering some eighteen pages, used a rectangular latitude and longitude grid system, with the latitude scales expanding as they receded from the equator towards the poles. He also devised a mathematical calculation to enable the mariner to find his longitude. However, it was far too complicated for practical use and it was not until the Englishman, Edward Wright, published his *Certaine Errors of Navigation* in 1599, that the navigator understood the benefits of adopting Mercator's theorem. The first British hydrographical department was established by the Admiralty in 1795 to produce accurate charts for use by the Navy, and their first catalogue, of some 736 charts, was published in 1825.

The instruments traditionally used in conjunction with charts were Napier's Bones, sectors, Gunter rules, single-handed dividers, parallel rulers and station pointers. To facilitate the extensive and cumbersome long multiplication and division required for some navigational calculations, John Napier, a Scottish laird, devised a series of logarithmic tables which he published in 1614. Napier also invented a set of ivory or wooden rods, punched with a series of numbers, intended as an alternative to the logarithmic tables, and housed in an accompanying case. These calculators, called 'Napier's Bones', were probably made throughout the seventeenth and early eighteenth centuries, although complete examples are now hard to find.

The 'sector' comprised two brass limbs, hinged together at one end and engraved with graduated lines of sines, tangents and other geometric functions. Using the sector in conjunction with a pair of dividers, calculations involving ratios and right-angled triangles could be made. The same results could also be achieved using the log scales and trigonometrical functions stamped on the wooden 'Gunter rule', as described in Gunter's book of 1623, and used by navigators until the end of the nineteenth century. Other instruments include: single-handed

Jesse Ramsden silver sextant

Instruments made from silver were produced in small numbers as their cost, relative to those made from brass, was high. They were made either as presentation pieces, or for some wealthy captain who wished to have an instrument of distinction.

Jesse Ramsden opened a workshop in the Haymarket in 1762 and introduced his dividing engine in 1775. This enabled him to divide accurately the scales on all types of instruments, a process previously performed by hand. However, since he had sold his invention to the Board of Longitude for the sum of £615, he was unable to take out a patent, which resulted in his competitors quickly building similar engines.

Ramsden produced some of the finest instruments during the last quarter of the 18th century; Captain James Cook used a Ramsden sextant on his second voyage.

Silver, ebony and glass, English, late 18th century, 30.5cm (12in) radius

56

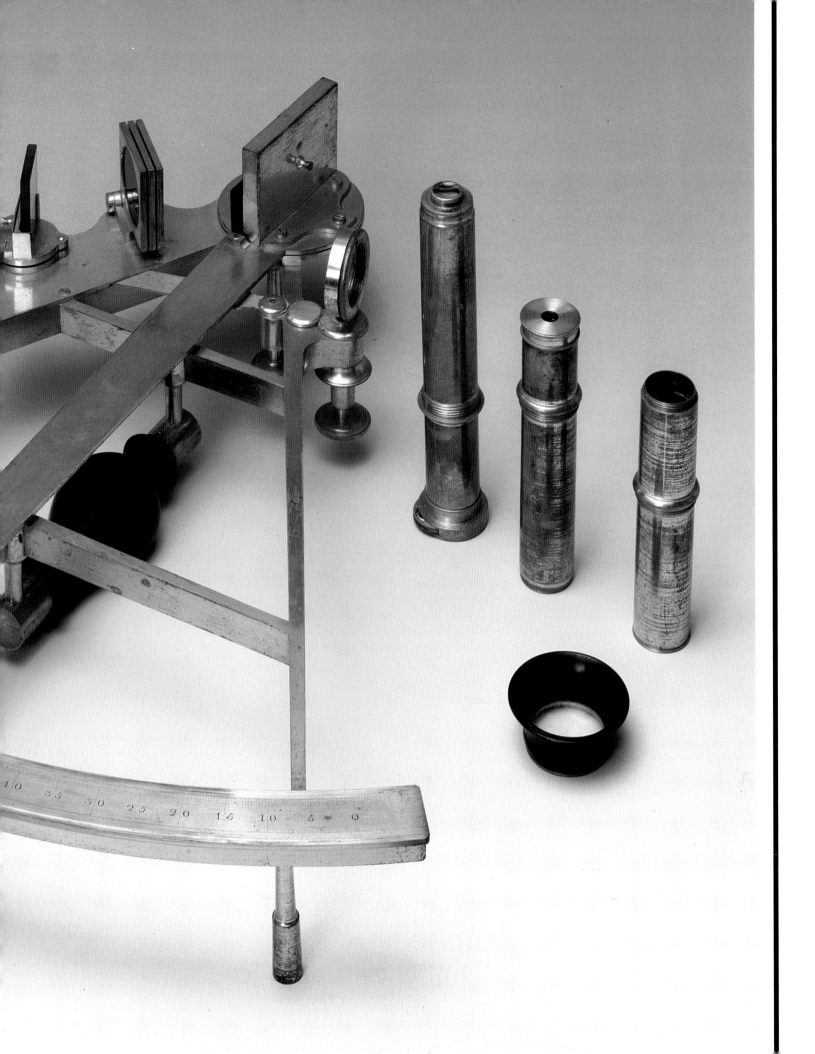

dividers, used for 'pricking out' a course on a chart, or measuring distances using a set of scales; the parallel ruler, introduced in the sixteenth century and whose design changed little until it was superseded by the wooden and metal rolling rulers; and the station pointer, invented by Murdoch Mackenzie in the 1780s and used for fixing the position of the ship when in view of the coast. This instrument consisted of a circular band of brass with central pivot and three adjustable arms. When laid on the chart, the three arms could be adjusted to align with known bearings, thus determining the position of the vessel.

Marine barometers were also made in considerable numbers during the nineteenth century. However, they would only have been reliable during fair weather since, despite being mounted in gimbals, the movement of the ship in rough weather would have made reading the scale somewhat difficult.

Globes were actively used as navigational aids at sea from as early as the sixteenth century until well into the eighteenth century, when it can be assumed that they took on the role of cabin decoration rather than as serious aids to navigation. Both celestial and terrestrial globes were constructed in the same manner: a number of printed ovoid-shaped segments, called 'gores', were applied to the sphere to make up the globe's surface. The spheres were initially made from solid pieces of wood, although later spheres tended to be made out of hollow papier mâché shells, coated with plaster. Since terrestrial globes avoided the problems of calculating the angles of projection, they remained popular with students of navigation long after Edward Wright published his *Certaine Errors of Navigation* in the late sixteenth century. Navigators relied on celestial globes to calculate their position on the oceans, by comparing their celestial observations with the model provided by the globe.

Globes vary in size from small pocket versions measuring only 3 or 4 inches in diameter, to those made for libraries which can measure up to 50 inches in diameter. As shops were unable to hold a vast stock of the larger globes due to restrictions on space, they tended to stock a selection of printed gores, from which clients could then make their selection. The gores might then be hand-coloured, applied to the spheres, and mounted within a brass meridian engraved with the latitude scale. They were then set upon a wooden stand made to the client's own specifications. As man's understanding of the constellations of the southern hemisphere improved, and as important voyages of discovery continued to find new lands, so these printed gores required regular updating. When dating globes, it is necessary, therefore, to take the published date of the gores as the earliest possible date of the globe, and to take into account any information later printed on the gores when determining the date of the stand. Typical eighteenth- and nineteenth-century tracks printed on gores are:

George Anson Circumnavigation of the globe 1740-44	George Vancouver Western Canada exploration 1791-95
Captain James Cook Circumnavigation of the globe 1768-71	Dumont d'Urville Circumnavigation of the globe 1826-29
Captain James Cook Circumnavigation of the globe 1772-75	Sir John Franklin North-West Passage 1845-47
Captain James Cook Pacific exploration 1776-79	
Completed by King 1780	

Other factors which determine the date of a globe are the developments in the knowledge of the coastlines of Australia and North America. California is shown as an island on gores dating from 1625 to as late as the 1780s, while some gores depict the island of Tasmania connected to the Australian mainland as late as 1792.

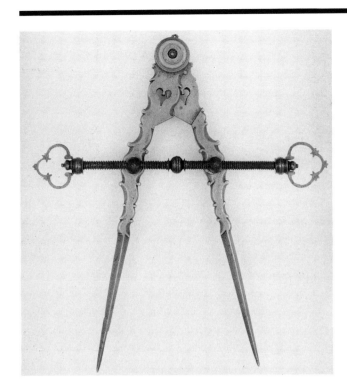

Iron and gilt-brass compass

This compass incorporates a central bar with middle wheel adjustment. By turning either of the trefoil-shaped bows, it is possible to vary the distance between the compass points, the interlocking leaves of which are pierced with heart-shaped decoration.

This type of compass might have been used by navigators, in conjunction with charts and scales, to determine distances.

Iron and gilt-brass, French, first half of the 17th century, 24cm (9½in) radius

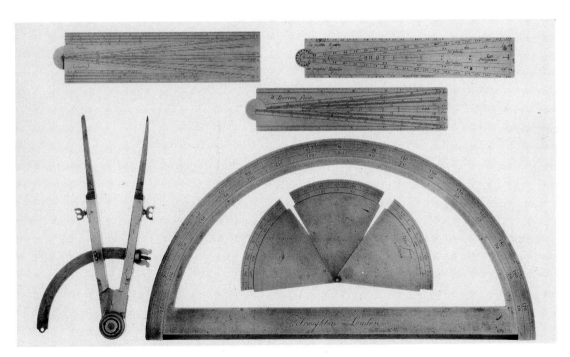

Six brass plotting instruments

The three sectors (top) are made by Pigeon of Lyon, France, and Edward Nairne and William Burton of England, and are engraved with similar trigonometrical scales. The dividers (left) were made in Germany during the late 17th century, and the large protractor (bottom right) was made by Edward Troughton of London. The adjustable example (bottom right) was made by the partnership of W. & S. Jones, also of London. Such instruments were used by draughtsmen, engineers and navigators.

Brass and iron, English, French and German, late 17th century to early 19th century, various sizes

Hughes & Son star globe

The celestial sphere is mounted within brass meridians and stowed in a mahogany case, which carries a set of instructions on the inside of the lid.

Mahogany, paper and brass, English, c.1920, the case 27cm (10½in) wide

Charles Price pocket terrestrial globe

This type of small-size globe was designed to be carried in the pocket, and was probably brought out by the owner as a model for use during discussions about the new worlds, then being discovered, or the stars. This example is housed in a spherical fish-skin case.

Paper, fish-skin and plaster, English, c.1730, 8cm (3in) diameter

Three marine barometers

J. Hughes marine barometer (left) with mahogany case and brass mercury tank, mounted with an ivory-backed thermometer.
Mahogany, brass, glass and ivory, English, mid-19th century, 93cm (36½in) high

Negretti & Zambra marine barometer (centre) with carved rosewood case, double ivory scale and front with marine sympiesometer, the whole mounted in gimbals.
Rosewood, brass, ivory and glass, English, c.1880, 100cm (39½in) high

Griffin & George Ltd, Kew Pattern marine barometer (right) with brass case and inset mercury thermometer with steel cistern cover and millibar scale.
Brass, steel and glass, English, c.1920, 93cm (36½in) high

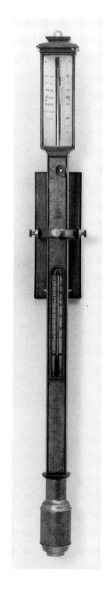

Henry Hughes marine barometer in gimbal mounts

This high-quality instrument has a satinwood-veneered case with inlaid ebony stringing. The ivory scale incorporates a tortoiseshell adjustment knob, and the front is inset with an alcohol thermometer. The whole is housed in brass gimbals and attached to a wall plaque inset with an ivory manufacturer's plate.

Satinwood, brass, glass and mercury, English, mid-19th century, 94cm (37in) high

Midshipman's pocket-book

These small pocket-books were filled with information important to the day-to-day running of a ship. This example includes signals, compass points, an almanac, tide times and navigation notes. They were also occasionally illustrated with portraits of boats and harbour scenes.

The majority of young men who wanted to become naval officers either joined the navy as a 'captain's servant', or were nominated by the First Lord of the Admiralty. They were automatically rated midshipmen after three years service, and sat an examination for the rank of lieutenant after six years. This method of entry continued until the establishment of the Britannia Naval College at Dartmouth in the middle of the 19th century.

Paper with leather binding, English, 19th century, small octavo

A pair of Isaac Habrecht terrestrial and celestial globes

Published by Johann Christoph Weigel of Nuremberg, the printed and hand-coloured gores carry a Latin inscription within a cartouche, which translates, in part, as 'Towards the arctic pole the last journey so far was that "Labour of Hercules" endured by the Englishman, Davis. Thus also the antarctic strait newly discovered by William Schouten, called "of Le Maire", is the furthest limit of navigation'. Both spheres are mounted in brass meridians and set within octagonal horizontal rings, applied with printed calendars and zodiac scales, and raised on four ebonized wood columns above oak bases.

Oak, paper and brass, German, late 17th century, the spheres 20cm (8in) diameter

The telescope

The telescope, and later the refracting telescope, was of immense importance to the development of navigation, and was adopted by pilots as soon as it came on to the market. The early navigators experienced a number of problems with regard to the practical application of telescopes for navigational purposes since, in order to obtain an effective magnification, it was necessary to have a long extending tube. This lengthy instrument became cumbersome and difficult to use against the motion of the ship. Moreover, the poor quality of the glass used in the lens led to a distortion of the image, known as 'chromatic aberration'. It was not until the middle of the eighteenth century, when the London instrument maker, John Dollond (1730-1820), patented and manufactured a new type of compound lens, that this distortion was corrected and it became possible to use a lens with a short focal length to obtain a large magnification.

Early telescopes were constructed from pasteboard tubes with turned wood or ivory mounts. However, these were replaced during the eighteenth century with those constructed of brass with an outer tube bound in leather, rayskin or wood.

Pierre Patroni ¾-inch refracting telescope

This Italian-made instrument is an example of an 18th-century hand-held refracting telescope which, instead of having the usual brass draw tubes, has draws made from pasteboard, covered with card. The lens and draw tube mounts are made from turned ivory, and the outer tube covering is of leather.

Ivory, pasteboard, glass and leather, Italian, early 18th century, extended length 88cm (34½in)

A pair of George Adams terrestrial and celestial globes

Globes of this type are more often found in country and town house libraries, than in a captain's cabin. The terrestrial globe often shows the paths of recent voyages of discovery, and both sets of gores are hand-coloured to enhance their overall attractiveness. Each sphere is mounted in a brass meridian and set within a horizontal ring, applied with a printed calendar and zodiac scale, upon a mahogany tripod stand.

Mahogany, brass, paper and plaster, English, late 18th century, the spheres 46cm (18in) diameter

Telescope walking stick

This unusual instrument was useful, perhaps, for those who took their daily exercise along the sea shore and who wished to be able to identify those ships visible to the eye. The top section of the stick unscrews and lifts up to reveal a two-draw telescope with leather outer cover and lens cap.

Bamboo, leather, glass and brass, English, third quarter of the 19th century, 76cm (30in) long

A pair of Steward presentation binoculars

Constructed as two telescopes mounted in parallel, with dual adjustment to the draw tubes for focusing, these were probably made for use on land, since the presentation mahogany case houses a tripod, which would have been impractical for use at sea due to the movement of the ship.

Mahogany, brass and glass, English, late 19th century, the case 36cm (14in) wide

Three 19th-century hand-held refracting telescopes

These are typical examples of 19th-century telescopes. All incorporate slightly different methods of construction (from top to bottom):

1½-inch refracting telescope made by Horne Thornthwaite & Hood, with six draws and a tube bound in horn.
Brass, glass and horn, English, mid-19th century, extended length 67.5cm (26½in)

1½-inch telescope made by Ebsworth of Fleet Street, with four silver-plated draws and a tube bound in ray-skin.
Silvered brass, glass and ray-skin, English, c.1825, extended length 1cm (28in)

2-inch telescope with four brass draws and a black-lacquered tube.
Brass, glass and black-lacquered wood, English, mid-19th century, extended length 102cm (40in)

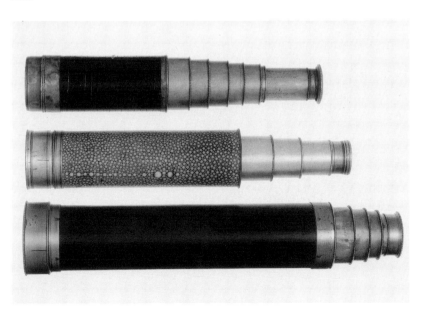

Fixtures and Fittings

THROUGHOUT the history of building wooden ships, there has been a strong tradition in Europe for embellishing and decorating various parts of the vessel. The craft of painting and carving wood reached the peak of its popularity during the seventeenth and eighteenth centuries, and can be divided broadly into bow and stern decoration and mast and rudder decoration. It is unfortunate that due to the ships of this period having only a short life span, and the carved wood being subjected to the rigours of the sea, very little early decoration survives today, although nineteenth-century material is still readily available.

One of the most famous ships to be built in England was the warship *Sovereign of the Seas*, designed by the leading architect, Phineas Pett, and launched in 1637. At the time, she was the most lavishly decorated ship ever to be built in a British shipyard. Her ornamentation was designed by Antony van Dyck, at that time court painter to King Charles I. The stern was carved and gilded with figures of Jupiter, Jason and Hercules, surrounding the goddess Victory, while the figurehead was carved in the form of King Edgar on horseback, tramping his opponents underfoot and surrounded by six allegorical figures representing the Virtues.

At the same time, in France, the Baroque sculptor, Pierre Puget, was commissioned to work on the great warships of the French Navy based at Toulon. However, with their massive allegorical figures and portraits of warriors, the ships became top-heavy and difficult to handle, sometimes endangering both the safety of the ship and its crew.

Figureheads

Throughout the seventeenth century, the most popular subject for a figurehead was the lion rampant, a symbol of aggression and power tamed by man. The English painted their figureheads gold, the Danes blue and the French red with gold manes. In common with Spanish carvers, the French sometimes painted their lion figureheads in all three colours. The larger and more important ships had increasingly elaborate figureheads. One such example was the *Prince Royal* of 1610, which carried a figure of St George slaying the dragon.

During the second half of the eighteenth century, the lion became unfashionable as a figurehead for warships and was replaced by carvings relating to the ship's name. An example was H.M.S. *Queen Charlotte* of 1790, which proudly displayed the figure of the Queen holding an orb and sceptre, standing below a canopy. She was supported by two cherubs and flanked by the figures of Britannia, Plenty, Prudence, Hope and Fortitude. This formidable figurehead displayed all the quality of craftsmanship and design inherent in the art of the wood carver. Such an expensive and complex group was typical of the type of figurehead reserved for first-rate ships-of-the-line, the lower ranks having to contend with single full- or half-length figures. In general, however, the subjects followed broadly Classical subjects: maidens, bearded and clean-shaved warriors and sea-gods. Ships named after eminent persons of the day often had a portrait of the celebrity, carved and painted in wood, adorning the bows.

The most noted and documented European carver was Johan Törnström (1743-1828) of

Limewood model figurehead of Neptune

This well-carved limewood and gesso model depicts Neptune wearing lose robes and a wreath of flowers on his head. He is standing on a hippocamp, which in turn is supported on a curved stand carved with arms, banners, a cross-staff, pikes and swords. The whole is mounted on a shaped stand with acanthus leaf decoration.

Wood and gesso, French, mid-18th century, 48cm (19in) high

Stockholm who, from 1782 to 1818, was the official carver at the Swedish naval dockyard at Karlskrona, where ten examples of his work can still be seen today. Influenced by the Swedish sculptor, Sergel, Törnström produced very large and vigorously carved full-length figures of Neo-Classical design. The tradition was continued by Emmanuel Törnström (1798-1863) who, although stylistically speaking was less free than his namesake, nevertheless produced fine work, including an impressive figurehead of the god, Odin, designed for the ship-of-the-line, *Skandinavien*, in 1860.

Following the battle of Copenhagen, shipbuilding in the Danish naval yards ceased until about 1814, when the job of designing and decorating men-of-war was given to the Academy of Fine Arts. The Danish had enormous respect for the style and quality of figureheads, and this is reflected in the highly complex and elaborate nature of their output during the mid-nineteenth century.

The first American wooden naval ships were those ordered in 1775 in anticipation of the forthcoming American Revolution, and many of their figureheads reflected that country's history and heroes. The privateer, *Rattlesnake*, of 1781, had a Red Indian figurehead, a theme which was to be repeated many times on the bows of American ships. The most important American figurehead carver was William Rush who, following his apprenticeship with the English carver, Edward Cutbush, established a business in his native city of Philadelphia in 1779. He designed the figurehead for one of the most important American warships, the frigate *Constitution* of 1797, which depicted a figure of Hercules standing on the rock of independence. Although he learnt his trade from an Englishman, he is probably best known for the way in which he broke away from the staid traditions of English carving, to produce original and lively works. The continuing influence of his work can be seen in the use of subjects such as American eagles, Indian figures and popular celebrities, like the singer Jenny Lind and the folk hero Davey Crocket, in the designs for figureheads of both naval and merchant ships during the nineteenth century.

*   *   *

In 1796, the Admiralty issued an order restricting the amount of money that could be spent on the installation of figureheads, and the *Centaur*, a seventy-four-gun ship-of-the-line of 1797, was one of the last ships to have a full-length figurehead. The abolition of this traditional form of ship decoration was intensely unpopular, both with seamen and dockyard workers, and many officials endeavoured to circumvent the ban. However, during the nineteenth century the beakhead, which supported the large, traditional figurehead, was superseded by the rounded bow, and figureheads were generally replaced with scrolls or shields. The number of men-of-war carrying figureheads continued to decline until the 1860s when, with the introduction of the straight-stemmed iron-clads in the 1860s, the traditional form of figurehead disappeared altogether. Two exceptions, however, were the sister ships *Warrior* and *Black Prince*, the first ever armoured battleships, launched in 1860. The *Warrior* was a full-rigged ship with twin funnels and coal-fired steam engine, capable of 14 knots. Her half-length figurehead depicted a finely carved, bearded Greek warrior with helmet, sword and shield. Her sister ship boasted a figure of the Black Prince, clad in chain-mail, making a backhanded sword stroke.

The French Navy also adopted the round bow during the Napoleonic Wars, and there-after the full-length figurehead made only sporadic appearances. Classical subjects were still

Carved oak figurehead of a lion

From the middle of the 16th century, the figurehead, usually a lion, was mounted almost horizontally. However, as ship design changed, and the beakhead gradually disappeared into the bow, so the figurehead assumed a more upright position and finally, by 1700 or so, was mounted perpendicular to the bow.

Oak, English, early 18th century, 109cm (43in) high

Ship's figurehead

The carved and painted wood figurehead depicts a Victorian gentleman with tousled hair and side whiskers, wearing a scarf and waistcoat, mounted on a scrolling support.

After a ship was broken up, the figurehead was often removed and either kept for interior decoration, placed in a museum or occasionally used for decorating the outside of a public house. This necessitated repainting the wood at regular intervals. These two illustrations show the same figurehead before (left), and after (right), careful removal of the paint to show some of the original patination and details.

Pine, English, mid-19th century, 97cm (39in) high

Massive carved wood figurehead from H.M.S. *Ajax*

This finely carved and painted figurehead represents Ajax, the giant Greek warrior. H.M.S. *Ajax* was built on the Thames at Blackwall in 1809, and was broken up in 1865. An extract from *Ships' Figureheads*, by Peter Norton, states 'though the Admiralty had issued an order in 1796 restricting the carved decoration on ships, a 3rd rate in 1806 such as the *Ajax* could be given such a splendid figurehead'.

Wood, English, 1806, 450cm (14ft 9in) high

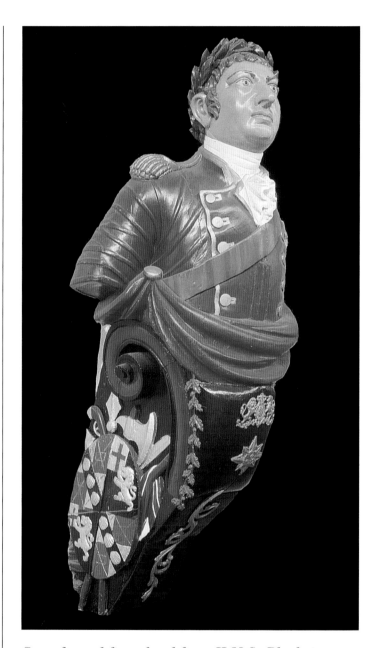

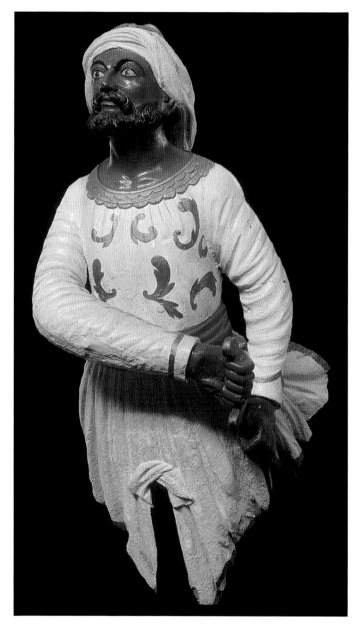

Carved wood figurehead from H.M.S. *Blenheim*

The figure, wearing a laurel wreath, is purported to be a portrait of the 1st Duke of Malborough, the victor of the Battle of Blenheim in 1704. The coats of arms, painted on either side of the base, represent those granted to the Spencer-Churchill family in 1733.

Wood, English, 1813, 305cm (10ft) high

Carved wood figurehead from H.M.S. *Himalaya*

Carved in the form of a Saracen-type warrior, this figurehead came off the *Himalaya*, a troopship built on the Thames at Blackwall in 1853. She served in the Crimea between 1854 and 1855, and was sunk in 1940 in the course of action during World War II.

Wood, English, 1853, 254cm (8ft 4in) high

predominant, although there are a small number of portrait busts in the Musée de la Marine in Paris which date from the 1820s and 30s.

During the eighteenth century merchant vessels followed their naval counterparts fairly closely in the design of their figureheads. The ships of the East India Company, for example, generally had lion figureheads. With the introduction of the clipper ship in the nineteenth century, with its sleek lines and sharp-raked stem, the wood carver's art experienced something of a renaissance. All manner of figures were used, either full- or half-length, with females more popular than males. By tradition, women were considered by seafarers to be unlucky. However, naked women were thought to be able to calm storms and therefore many female figureheads have one or both breasts bared. With the introduction of steam power in the mid-nineteenth century, and the corresponding changes in hull shape, especially the loss of the bowsprit, figureheads began to disappear from merchant ships, although a few of the smaller masted sailing ships continued to carry them until well into the twentieth century.

Gear, furniture and fittings

It was not until the nineteenth century that furniture was designed specifically for use at sea, and crews' quarters were generally of simple construction. However, the more lavish accommodation allowed to the Captain was often furnished with chairs, tables and globes, all of which could be transferred easily to a house on shore.

Bridge furnishings included such items as the floor-standing telegraph, which transmitted directions to the engine room. The 'Full Ahead', 'Astern' and other commands were painted on a white enamel dial. The handle and pointer were then turned to the appropriate command, which was repeated, via connecting wires, on a similar dial in the engine room. This action was accompanied by the ringing of a bell to draw attention, and there was sometimes a speaking tube connecting both operations rooms.

The ship's wheel, or 'helm', was normally constructed from a hardwood such as mahogany, and strengthened with brass bands and a central boss. The frame consisted of eight spokes, at the ends of which were shaped handholds. The helm was connected to the ship's steering gear – which controlled the rudder – by means either of cables and pulleys, a screw mechanism, or pneumatics. Wheels varied in diameter from anything between two or three feet, to as much as six feet for those on the fastest clippers, where two large wheels were often mounted on the same axis. On smaller sailing vessels the rudder was controlled by a wooden tiller, and this was often carved and decorated with twisted patterns and knots to produce a decorative, yet practical, fitting.

From the beginning of the eighteenth century, large stern lanterns were used to illuminate ships, and these were mounted with bull's-eye or convex lens panels to intensify the light supplied by the oil-lamp inside. Constructed from gilded wood, they were generally lined with metal to reduce the risk of fire. During the nineteenth century navigation lights became more uniform, and international regulations were established stating that a white light should be placed on the mast, red and green sidelights to port and starboard respectively, and a white light fixed to the stern. Made from copper and brass, with thick-ribbed and curved glass lenses, such lights can often be seen today, wired for electricity and displayed in surroundings such as fish restaurants, theme wine bars and public houses, often together with heavy brass portholes, or scuttles.

Made out of pine, the sailor's sea chest was usually a crude affair, slightly broader at the base, for greater stability, and with rope handles at the sides. Used for storing clothes and personal possessions, the inside of the lid was sometimes painted with a simple ship's portrait.

Little remains today of the type of furniture made specifically for use on board ship. However, examples of the 'saloon chairs' can still be found, with curved backrails and circular seats mounted on cast-iron tripod bases. Other examples include folding wooden cruise ship deckchairs and cabin wash-stands with folding wash-basin, water reservoir and drainage tank.

The Captain's quarters on board a sailing ship were located on the starboard side of the poop, and often contained an office, sleeping cabin and bathroom. The furniture would have

Sternboad from the Danish ketch *J M Nielsen*

This slightly curved sternboard is carved from pine, with raised lettering and painted decoration. The ketch was wrecked off the north Cornish coast during the late 19th century.

Pine, Danish, late 19th century, 219cm (86in) long

Carved wood sternboard from the barge of Admiral Collier

This ornate sternboard is delicately carved in relief with figures of angels and cherubs, fruits, swags and acanthus leaves flanking Admiral Collier's coat of arms, above which is a ribbon bearing the motto 'PERSEVERE'.

Collier was personally chosen by Admiral Lord Nelson to act as his midshipman. He rose steadily through the ranks and was promoted to Admiral during the 1820s.

Mahogany, English, c.1830, 254cm (100in) long

Mast wortel

This type of ornamental carving was popular on Dutch vessels during the 18th century. Designed to be attached to the top of the mast, this example is carved with diminishing tiers of figurative and floral designs.

Oak, Dutch, 18th century, 125cm (49in) high

Chadburn's ship's telegraph

The bridge telegraph has an operating handle which, when turned to the desired command, transmits this command, via a system of wires, to the engine room, where another telegraph indicates the same command on a similar dial. The command is accompanied by the ringing of a bell to alert the crew of the engine room that an order has been given.

Brass, English, early 20th century, 117cm (46in) high

Ship's wheel

This eight-spoked mahogany wheel with brass hub, is mounted on a turned brass column with a direction indicator set at the top.

Mahogany and brass, English, early 20th century, 137cm (51in) high

included a simple bed, with clothes drawers in the base, and a series of gimbal-mounted oil-lamps, fitted with smoke shields, attached to the bulkheads. There would also have been some form of writing desk fixed to the bulkhead, and a cupboard for housing all the ship's documents, including ship's logs, letters and charts, together with a locker for the safe-keeping of chrono-meters and other navigational instruments. Other fittings would probably have included a mercury thermometer, again mounted in gimbals to keep it upright, an aneroid barometer, and mounts for holding a telescope and rifle.

Other more utilitarian fittings were wooden water buckets, located throughout the ship in case of fire, and fresh water casks, of supreme importance aboard ship, located in the central part of the vessel and made from caulked planks and brass rings, similar to a cooper's work. The British Navy's traditional tot of rum, or 'grog', was again kept in a wooden cask, this time secured with a lock, and many were applied with the words 'GOD SAVE THE KING' in brass lettering. Grog was a mixture of three parts water to one part rum, and was always concocted in the presence of

A pair of caryatid female figures from a French man-of-war

These chestnut-wood figures, looking to left and right, are carved with long robes, scrolls at thigh height and wear lead necklaces and bracelets. The bases are carved with floral and leaf decoration.

Chestnut-wood, French, early 19th century, 218cm (86in) high

A pair of Ray & Co. ship's telegraphs

On some larger types of ship, the bridge was fitted with two telegraphs or, occasionally, the ship had two bridges, each with its own telegraph. Two telegraphs were used either when commands needed to be issued very quickly, or when they constantly changed during complicated manoeuvring, such as docking.

Brass, English, early 20th century, 120cm (47in) high

Ship's wheel

This mahogany wheel has an inset brass band and a central brass hub inscribed 'BROWN BROS. & Co. Ltd EDINBURGH'. The wheel is connected by wires, or gears, to the ship's rudder, so ensuring that the wheel and the rudder turn in the same direction. The reverse is true of the tiller, which moves in the opposite direction to the rudder. Until World War I, orders given to the helmsman remained applicable to the tiller instruction rather than the wheel. For example, if the order was given to turn 'starboard 10' then the helmsman turned the wheel 10 degrees to port and the ship's head moved to port. By the 1930s, however, all nations had changed this policy and the order to turn starboard meant the ship turned in that direction, thus removing the anomaly.

Mahogany and brass, Scottish, late 19th century, 184cm (72in) diameter

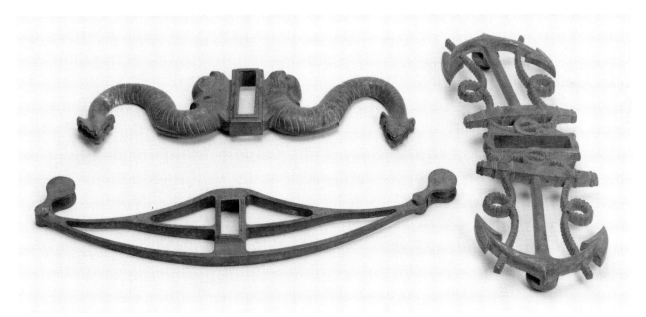

Three cast-brass rudder heads

In small vessels, the top of the rudder was sometimes fitted with a brass head, at either end of which was a block through which the controlling rope was passed. Using the rope and rudder head, the vessel could be steered either by hand, or by connecting the ropes to the steering gear and a wheel.

These three examples include designs incorporating stylized fish and double anchors.

Brass, English, late 19th century, the largest 48cm (19in) wide

an officer in order to prevent unscrupulous pursers from over-diluting the tot. It was issued on a daily basis at noon and 6.00pm, with one pint to every adult man and half a pint for boys. The evening issue of grog was abolished in the Royal Navy in 1824 and the daily ration reduced to one gill in 1850. Although chief and petty officers drank their rum undiluted, for all other ratings the ration was watered down until 1970, when it was discontinued altogether.

The ships's bell was made from brass, with the name of the vessel and launch date traditionally engraved on the side. For this reason they became highly prized mementoes of service on board a ship. The bell was normally located near the helmsman and was struck, using a clapper and rope handle, to mark the passage of time on board. The day was divided into six watches of four hours each; however, in order to prevent the same crew member keeping the same watch each day, the watch between 4.00pm and 8.00pm was divided into two parts, known respectively as the first and last dog watch. Within each watch the time lapse was marked by the bell every half-hour, one at the end of the first half-hour and eight bells at the end of the watch. Seamen traditionally referred to hours as bells, and thus, for example, they would refer to a quarter-past one as fifteen minutes past two bells.

Carved oak tiller

The handle of this tiller is carved in the form of a clenched hand and the shank with a spiral rope design. The head is carved with a laurel wreath inset with a clenched fist above a scroll inscribed 'E PLURIBUS UNUM' beneath a cartouche inscribed 'CAESAR WISCASSET'.

Oak, English, mid-19th century, 100cm (39in) long

Carved mahogany tiller

The shank of this tiller is carved with an unusual spiral rope design, terminating in a Turk's head knot handle.

Mahogany, English, 19th century, 74cm (29in) long

Helmsman's stand

Whilst on deck, the helmsman was exposed to spray and wind, as well as the violent movement of the ship in stormy weather. This type of stand would have provided him some protection from being swept off his feet, since the shaped back would have offered support. Water washing across the deck would have fallen through the duck-board at the helmsman's feet.

Brass and pine, English, late 19th century, 140cm (55in) high

East India Company chest-on-stand

The hardwood chest is applied with beaten brass panels and half spheres, and bears the letters 'VOC' on the matching low stand. The sides of the chest are applied with brass carrying handles.

Hardwood and brass, Anglo-Indian, late 18th century, 82cm (32½in) wide

Two pairs of navigation lamps

Each pair contains a coloured lens for port and starboard. The oil-burning lamps are housed in copper and brass cases.

Copper, brass and glass, English, late 19th century, the larger 41cm (16in) high

Ship's foghorn

This 'Norwegian Pattern' foghorn has a copper trumpet, and is housed in a pine case with a crank handle at the side.

Foghorns were fitted to larger ships, but small craft carried portable horns, such as this, and these were used to warn of the vessel's presence.

Pine, copper and leather, English, early 20th century, 58cm (23in) long

Games table from H.M.S. *Black Prince*

The oak table is inset with a glass top, the underside of which is painted with a checkers board, Prince of Wales feathers, a crown and a banner bearing the name of the ship.

Oak and glass, English, late 19th century, 48cm (19in) square

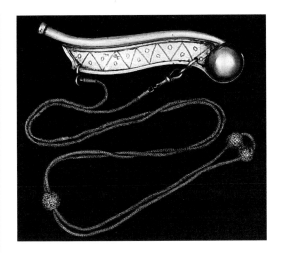

Boatswain's whistle or pipe

The shaped silver pipe has engraved decoration and is attached to a silver neck chain. The simple pipe was originally used by the boatswain's mate to pipe orders throughout the warship. The boatswain, pronounced 'bo'sun', was the officer in charge of the sails and rigging on board a sailing ship of the navy and, in addition, was also on charge of all work on deck under the supervision of the deck officer.

Today, the whistle has been superseded by the tannoy, although the instrument is still used in the Royal Navy for piping on board visiting commanding officers and other dignitaries.

Silver, French, dated 1789, 16cm (6¼in) long

Royal Navy grog barrel

This grog barrel is made of pine, and is lettered 'THE KING'. The hinged lid has a brass handle and a star-shaped surround.

Also known as a 'grog tub', the cut-down barrel contained the watered down rum that was issued daily to the crew on board Royal Navy ships. The formula of three parts water to one of rum was always mixed in the presence of the officer in charge, in order to ensure that the concoction was not over diluted.

The Royal Navy ceased the issue of grog in 1970.

Pine and brass, English, early 20th century, 72cm (28in) high

Two ship's saloon chairs

These kinds of upholstered chairs were mounted on cast-iron stands and bolted to the floor. The chair could swivel about a vertical axis, ensuring the occupant remained upright in heavy seas. Both of these chairs are carved in mahogany, with the back splat of the right-hand example bearing the initials of the shipping company.

Mahogany, cast-iron, cane and red velvet, English, 1880-1900, the larger 89cm (35in) high

Medicine chest

The combination of poor diet and heavy work load on board ship meant that the average seaman might regularly need the attentions of a doctor who, in general, was at the next port of call. However, most ships had some form of medicine chest which would have contained many powders and ointments for the relief of such minor ailments as constipation, and stronger drugs such as laudanum, a tincture of opium, for the relief of intense pain.

Fruitwood, pewter, glass and silvered metal, probably Portuguese, late 18th century, 16.5cm (6½in) high

Two ships' badges

The badge on the left is of carved and painted wood, and bears the inscription 'HEAVENS LIGHT OUR GUIDE'; the other, of painted and cast-brass, is inscribed 'MAGNIFICENT'.
By the beginning of this century badges were made from cast metal and designed as heraldic or decorative devices associated with the ship's name, to be displayed on board in the mess room, or in some other prominent location.

Wood and brass, English, early 20th century, the larger 23cm.(9in) diameter

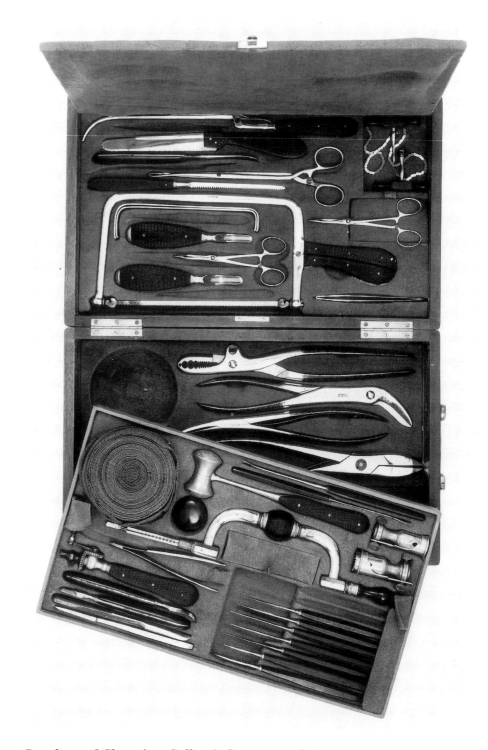

Cased set of Charrière Collin & Cie surgeon's instruments

The case is fitted with instruments for amputation, trepanning and minor operations. Naval surgeons had to endure harsh conditions while performing their duties. They had little room either for their equipment, or for performing operations, since their allotted space was often below the waterline with no ventilation and little lighting.
The St Vincent reforms of 1799, required all naval surgeons to carry a set of pocket instruments with them at all times, a rule not finally abolished until the 1930s.

Ebony, steel, cloth and mahogany, French, mid-19th century, the case 39.5 x 24cm (15½ x 9½in)

Ship's saloon clock from the P. & O. brig *Delhi*

This clock contains an eight-day movement. Its silvered metal dial is encased in gilt-brass and engraved 'P & O.S.N.Co.' and 'DELHI'. The whole is supported on a short gilt-brass column with classical caryatid and scrolling acanthus leaf decoration.

Gilt brass, steel, glass and brass, English, late 19th century, 82cm (32½in) high

Seaman's painted chest

This pine chest is painted with a portrait of the steam and sail ship *Arcadia*. Such chests would have contained clothes and other personal items belonging to the sailor. Although few genuine examples are found with painted lids, recently there has been a trend for producing modern paintings on old chests. These can be easily identified by their very gaudy colours, large lettering, giving the name of the ship, and a date. Furthermore, the new paint often gives off a strong odour.

Pine, English, third quarter of the 19th century, 46 cm (18in) wide

Silver arm badge for the Commercial Dock Company, Rotherhithe

The oval plate is engraved with the Company name, together with a scene of a ship with furled sails entering a dock. The reverse carries the London Assay marks for 1820-21 and the makers mark 'IP'.

These types of badges were worn on the arm by watermen. In addition to serving as an identification device, they also offered some protection against seizure by the Press Gang.

Silver, London 1821-22, 9.5 x 8.2cm (3¾ x 3in)

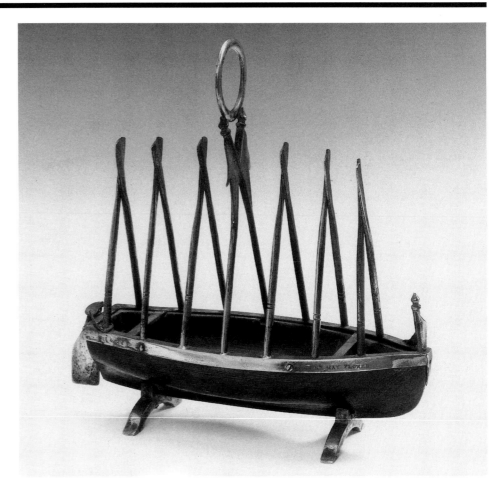

Boating toast rack

The shaped oak hull, bearing the name 'The Mayflower', is mounted with a silver rudder, a pennant, six pairs of crossed oars and a pair of crossed masts attached to a loop handle.

Silver and oak, English, early 20th century, 20cm (8in) long

Cabin wash-stand

The mahogany cabinet has a hinged flap at the front which pulls down to reveal a painted tin sink with a shelf and mirror above. The base contains a reservoir for the water.

Mahogany and brass, English, early 20th century, 188cm (74in) high

The speaking trumpet from H.M.S. *Victory*

The tapering copper trumpet is engraved on the side 'VICTORY 100 Guns Launched at Chatham 1765 Flagship of Keppel at Ushany 1778 Kempenfelt 1781 Howe at Gibraltar 1782 Hood at Toulon 1783 Jervis at St Vincent, 1797, Nelson at Trafalgar, 1805, Saumarez in Baltic, 1812, Paid Off, 1812', and around the bell 'this speaking trumpet was on Nelson's Flagship Victory at Trafalgar 21 Oct. 1805'.

Brass, English, 18th century, 64cm (25in) long

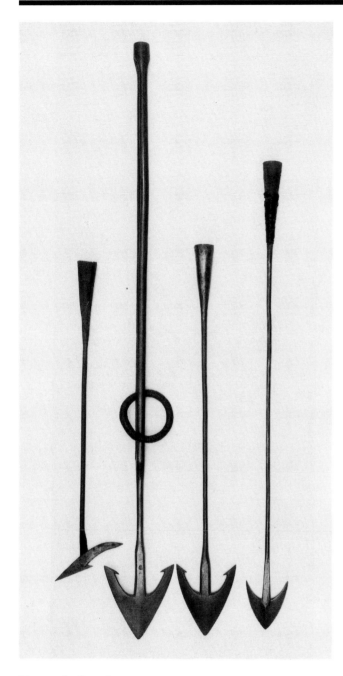

Ship's bell

The cast-brass bell, inscribed 'KAMMERUN HAMBERG', has an iron clapper with a rope handle, and is mounted on a later wooden stand.

Brass, iron and rope, German, late 19th century, mouth 43cm (16½in) diameter

Diver's helmet

This type of helmet was designed to be used in conjunction with Augustus Siebe's diving suit, developed in the late 19th century. Air was provided by a hand-cranked pump, operated by the crew of a support vessel, and supplied to the diver via a hose. The diver wore a lead-weighted belt and boots to ensure he remained submerged.

Brass, copper and glass, English, early 20th century, 43cm (17in) high

Four whaling harpoons

The toggle harpoon (left), together with the three fixed barbs head harpoons, would have been used with an attached line for catching and securing whales. During the early years of whaling, hand-held harpoons were used by a whaler standing at the bows of a large rowing boat. Such scenes are often found on scrimshawed whales' teeth, often with several boats chasing one or more whales. Later on in the 19th century, harpoon guns were introduced.

Iron, English and American, 19th century, the longest 130cm (51in)

Naval weapons

There has been violence at sea since man first took to sailing the oceans. Piracy, skirmishes and full-scale battles involving hundreds of ships have occurred since the time of the Armada. Sailors have always been prepared to defend themselves and few ships sailed without some weaponry aboard. Weapons from before the seventeenth century are rare and the majority of surviving pieces date from the eighteenth century and later.

Most ships carried some form of cannon, many examples of which have survived and can be seen today decorating the grounds of yacht clubs, naval establishments and maritime museums. Many of the smaller cannon were originally fitted on swivels to increase their arc of fire. This type of swivel cannon was common until the seventeenth century, when the improving skills of craftsmen allowed for larger guns to be cast. These were commonly mounted on stepped carriages, which enabled the cannon to travel backwards and thereby absorb the recoil when fired. The iron used to cast the cannons was subject to the corrosive effects of sea water and they were therefore given a thick coat of black paint in order to afford some protection. Later examples were cast in brass and these are of particular attraction to collectors. Other features worth noting are the casting of the sovereign's coat of arms and the date, both of which add to the value.

From the seventeenth century, pistols and muskets were increasingly supplied to ships, and gradually set patterns of naval design were developed. Many of these pistols were fitted with a belt hook, a flat bar fitted to one side of the wooden body, which enabled the pistol to be hooked on to a belt or trouser band, so freeing the sailor's hands for close combat. Some pistols can be found applied with the name of the ship, and with letters and numbers punched in dots on the butt caps, thus identifying where the pistol was to be stored.

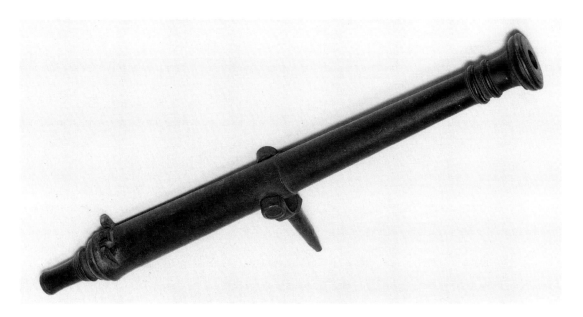

Bronze lantaka

The bronze barrel, cast with muzzle and twin reinforcement rings, is mounted in a trunnion above swivel pin. This cannon possesses an internal back-sight and a top vent.

Bronze, Indonesian, 19th century, 62cm (24½in) long

Six swords presented to Captain W. Moffat

William Moffat was Captain in the service of the East India Company from 1799. He sailed to Bengal and Bombay in 1800, to Madras in 1801 and to China in 1803. Moffat was instrumental in fighting off four attacking French men-of-war when the East India fleet was sailing home from China in 1804. This rare collection of presentation swords includes one given to him by his French adversary, Captain Dutorte in 1800; one given to him by M. C. Hindostan and Captain William Mackintosh in 1798, and one given to him by the Bombay Insurance Society for his role in the conflict with the French in 1804.

The curved blade of the Dutorte sword is inscribed, in English and French, 'By the French Captain John Dutorte Officers and Crew of the Private French SHIP of War General Marlartique to the English CAPTAIN W MOFFAT as a token of esteem for his kindness and Humanity when Prisoners on Board his SHIP the PHOENIX in November 1800. From their Prison Fort William Calcutta December 15th 1800'.

Ivory, gilt-brass, steel and leather, late 18th and early 19th centuries, the longest 66.5cm (34in)

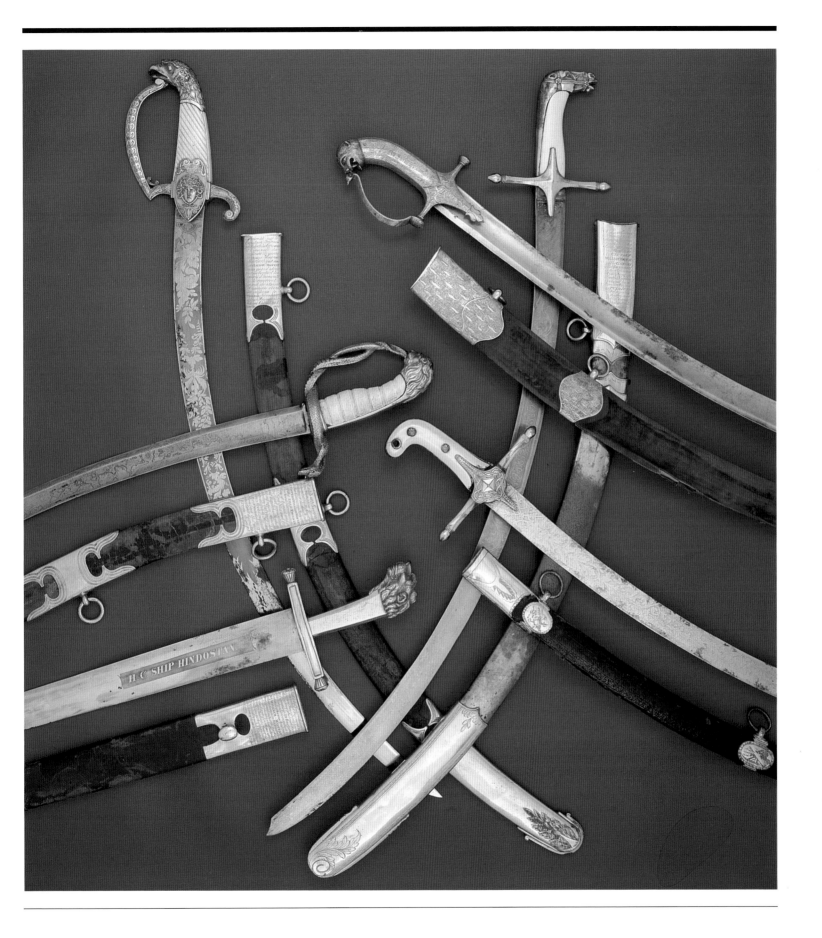

Naval battles could involve ships closing alongside, when the crews crossed over to the enemy's deck and indulged in hand-to-hand combat. In addition to pistols, sailors would probably have carried cutlasses. These swords were not decorative, having straight, single-edged blades with a simple guard for the hand. Other weapons in the seaman's armoury included the boarding pike, intended to ward off boarders, and the boarding axe. Used both as a tool and a weapon, its prime purpose was for dealing with fallen rigging, with the spike being used to pull clear burning debris.

Most officers would have owned at least two swords in the late eighteenth and early nineteenth centuries: a dress sword, whose style was dictated by regulations; and a fighting sword, which would have been chosen by the officer. Many officers also carried a small dagger-like knife, known as a 'dirk'. Swords with curved blades were common, although they tended to be personal weapons, since they were not, at that time, standard naval issue. Much later on in the nineteenth century, a formal pattern for curved-blade swords was designed for midshipmen in the British Navy, and examples are still readily available today.

In the early eighteenth century it was the custom to present decorative swords to Captains as a mark of appreciation. They were sometimes made from expensive materials, often with ornate embellishments, and invariably had a presentation script engraved on the blade or scabbard. The Lloyd's Patriotic Fund presented such swords to naval officers who had performed a particular act of bravery, and the combination of high-quality construction, together with historical interest, means that they are keenly collected today.

The design of naval swords varied quite considerably, although many countries used the common motif of a fouled anchor of fluked design, with a rope entwining the shank, engraved or etched on to the blade.

Two Venetian bronze cannon

The top cannon has centrally mounted sights and is cast with the lion of St Mark on the breech. The upper section of the barrel bears the letter 'P' above an oval cartouche. The holes next to the vent are for the attachment of a flintlock.

Bronze, Venetian, 18th century, 100.5cm (39½in) long; 7.5cm (3in) bore

Long flintlock sea service pistol

The barrel, with pistol bore and lock, is inscribed 'TOWER' and bears a crown over the initials 'GR'. The full-length stock has regulation brass furniture, a belt-hook and a brass-tipped wooden ramrod.

Mahogany, brass and iron, English, c.1800, 49cm (19¼in) long

Brass signal cannon

The barrel of this cast-brass cannon is moulded at the muzzle, fitted with an elevation screw, and mounted on a painted iron carriage with four cast-iron wheels.

Iron and brass, 19th century, 1-inch calibre, overall length 71cm (28in)

Marine Arts and Crafts

IN ADDITION to the arts of ship painting and model building, there is a wide range of decorative arts and crafts executed, with varying degrees of skill, by seamen and those associated with ships and the sea.

The best examples of the mariner's craft have all the naïve charm and decorative appeal of the most respected forms of folk art and, over the last twenty years, this field has seen a dramatic increase in numbers of collectors.

While seafarers were generally extremely busy when leaving or entering port, or during outbreaks of inclement weather, there were periods, especially on long voyages, when those off watch had time to kill. In these circumstances the average seaman passed the time by pursuing fairly simple activities such as gambling, or even fighting. However, certain of them turned their attentions to handicrafts. Using their own crudely made tools, or those borrowed from the ship's carpenter, these seamen fashioned a wealth of small items and furniture, either for their own use, or as presents for those at home.

Scrimshaw

The thriving whaling industry that existed in the nineteenth century, worked by the whaling fleets from the east coast of North America and several British ports, produced both the raw material and the craftsmen for an exquisite art form known as 'scrimshaw'. The name, the origins of which remain uncertain, refers both to the act of making a piece of decorative ware using whale products, and to the completed art form. The earliest reference to the art of scrimshaw, appears in the logbook of the brig *By Chance*, operating out of Dartmouth, Massachusetts, and now housed at the New Bedford Whaling Museum. The entry for 20 May 1826 reads, 'All these 24 hours small breezes and thick foggy weather, made no sale [sic]. So ends this day, all hands employed Scrimshanting'. Although the earliest recorded date for a scrimshawed whale's tooth is believed to be 1821, there can be little doubt that the craft was being practised as early as the eighteenth century.

The raw materials used were whales' teeth, bones and baleen, a dark coloured material taken from the roof of the mouth of a sperm whale, as well as walrus tusks, known as 'morse' ivory. The whalemen engraved various designs on to these materials, including memorials to the dead, valentines for their sweethearts and various scenes depicting the homestead. More often than not, the scenes were of whalers, ships and the sea.

Being naturally ridged, the whale's tooth initially has to be scraped smooth. Using both his jack-knife and sailor's needle, the scrimshander would then 'prick out', or outline, the design upon the surface. Sometimes a picture from a book or periodical was applied to the surface and the outline transferred to the ivory by pricking through the paper. The engraving was then completed by joining the dots and the lines made more visible by applying them with black ink. If ink was not available, then tar, soot or lampblack was used to enhance the outline. Occasionally pieces of scrimshaw are discovered with red or green ink details, giving an overall

Prisoner-of-war bone 'Spinning Jenny' automaton

This complex toy has a hand-cranked and geared mechanism which operates the movement of the two Breton ladies seated at their spinning wheels, the baby rocking in its cradle, and the two dancing couples. Mounted on the base are four sentries, each holding a rifle and accompanied by a spotted dog.

Bone and straw, French, early 19th century, 18cm (7in) high

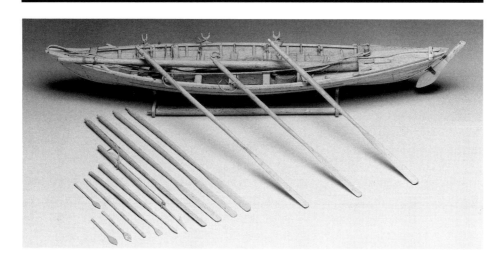

Whalebone model of a whaling boat

This clinker-built model is fitted with thwarts, mast and rigging, oars and rowlocks, rudder, harpoons with rope and rope basket, flensing knife and other whaling instruments.

Whalebone, English or American, 20th century, 46cm (18in) long

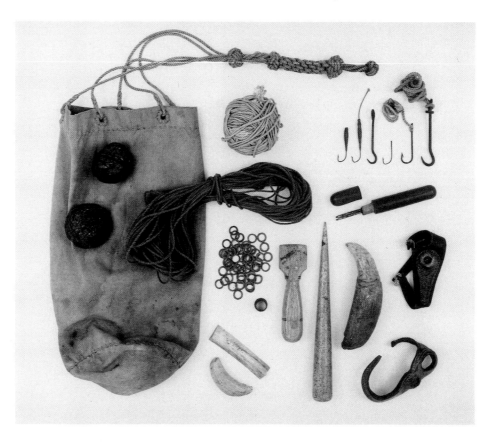

Canvas bag of whaleman's tools

Included in this bag are a seam rubber and fid made from whalebone, a set of needles in a bamboo case, two leather stitching harnesses and two undecorated whales' teeth.

19th century, various materials and sizes

dramatic effect to their design, while others are carved in relief to give an added dimension to the art form.

Whalebone could also be decorated in a similar style. Using what is called a 'panbone', or a large, flat piece of whalebone, the scrimshander could create much larger scenes, including whole whaling fleets and depictions of the chase. The bone could also be turned on a simple lathe, producing a long tapering rod, which, when mounted with a decorative handle, created an attractive type of walking stick.

Apart from the engraving of whales' teeth, other types of scrimshaw included the 'stay busk' and 'jagging wheel'. The busk was a flat piece of whalebone, measuring about 1 inch by 8 or 9 inches, engraved with sentimental or romantic motifs and verses. It was given to the seaman's sweetheart and worn as part of the bodice stay, very close to the wearer's heart. Decoration sometimes included whaling scenes or, more commonly, figures of either the sailor or his lady-love, along with lines like 'When this you see, remember me', and the initials of the owner, sometimes with a date.

Unlike the intimate stay busk, the jagging wheel, or pie crimper, was a useful kitchen tool for the housewife or fiancée. The delicate design of some examples reveal much about the craftsman's artistic skills and indicate, perhaps, how the whaleman's heart was swayed by the culinary skills of his partner. The basic construction of the crimper, or 'jagger', consisted of a small wheel, with either a thin edge or a zig-zag design engraved on the circumference. This was mounted on a shaped handle and used for cutting pastry and crimping and fluting the pie-crust edging so popular in New England cooking. The more complicated crimpers had handles shaped in the form of animals or other designs, with multiple wheels and fork-mounted handles to perforate the pie crust and allow steam to escape.

Pie crimpers were not the only types of scrimshaw made specifically for domestic use. While baking, the whaleman's wife, or sweetheart, could measure out ingredients using a whalebone scoop, or roll pastry using a whalebone and wood rolling pin. Additional practical articles included whalebone or ivory apple peelers, knife boxes, butter moulds, clothes-pegs and napkin rings. Other domestic chores performed by the whaleman's true-love were sewing and mending, and the scrimshander contrived many articles to assist her in her work. These included carved ivory needle cases, wood and bone work boxes, bodkins and darning eggs. One of the most attractive types of scrimshaw was the woolwinder, or 'swift'. Used in place of the more traditional method of winding wool, around a partner's outstretched hands, the swift was an expanding reel of ivory, baleen, whalebone and wood, fastened by rivets and ribbons and pivoted on a stand or table clamp. The hank of wool was placed around the reel, and this was then revolved so the yarn could be wound into a ball at the correct tension. Many swifts were constructed from over 100 individual pieces, and they can vary in height from no more than a couple of inches for lace work swifts, to perhaps 15 or 18 inches for those designed to be used with the heaviest yarns. The larger examples can also be found mounted on a box, inlaid with coloured marquetry, with a drawer below for storing accessories.

A word of warning to those who might wish to collect scrimshaw. There are many apparent examples of decorated whales' teeth, porpoise jaws, walrus tusks and associated articles on the market, which are, in fact, made from injection moulded resin and these should not be confused with the real article. The replicas are much heavier than the original, having a warm, greasy feel to the surface and lacking the deep gorge at the root of the tooth. Many bear dates from the early

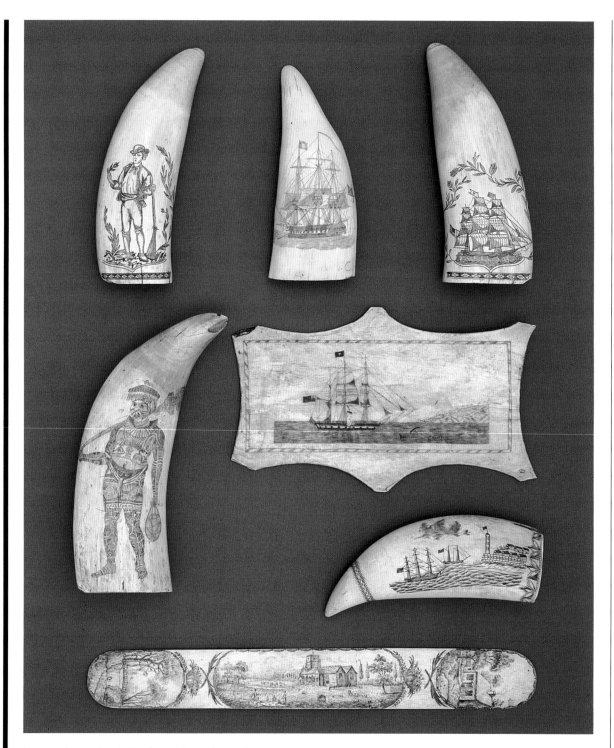

Scrimshawed whales' teeth and panbones

The top row of this illustration comprises a pair of teeth, engraved and coloured respectively with portrait of a settler holding a flintlock rifle and a three-masted ship in full sail, flanking another tooth engraved with a British warship. Below these is a very large tooth engraved with a study of a richly decorated Polynesian native, together with a panbone decorated with a whaling scene.

The busk at the bottom is decorated with a scene of a churchyard with group of picnickers, on either side of which are small vignettes of rural scenes. Above this there is a tooth engraved with a marine scene depicting two ships entering a harbour.

Whalebone and whale ivory, English and American, 19th century, various sizes

Scrimshawed whale's tooth attributed to Edward Burdett

Edward Burdett is considered to be one of the earliest American scrimshanders, and there are six known examples signed by him. His style is quite distinctive: vine borders, deeply gouged details, stylized seas, and the use of red sealing wax.

Little is known about Burdett's life, although his maiden voyage on the Nantucket whaleship *Foster* (1822-24) is recorded in a fellow shipmate's journal. Other voyages are gleaned from the scenes depicted on the teeth themselves. In 1833, while in close pursuit of a harpooned whale, Burdett became entangled in the whale line and was yanked overboard and drowned at the tragically early age of twenty-seven.

Whale ivory, American, c.1828, 19cm (7½in) long

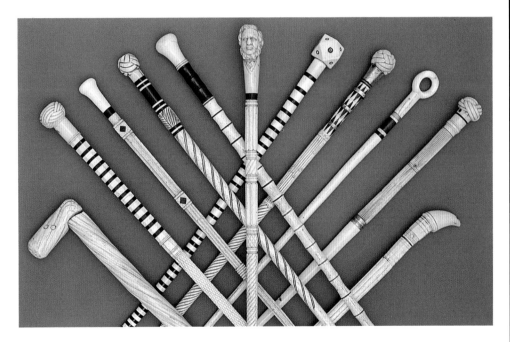

Eleven marine ivory and bone walking sticks

These canes are variously constructed from bone, which can be identified by the dark flecks in the grain, and whale ivory, which is creamy in colour and of dense grain. The near-black material used for the decoration is a flexible bone, called baleen, which comes from the plates in the mouth of the baleen whale used to trap the small organisms which form the whale's food. The stick on the far left hand side is made from the spiral horn of the narwhal which develops from one, or both, of its two teeth.

Whalebone, whale ivory, baleen and narwhal ivory, English and American, mid-19th century, the longest 90cm (36in)

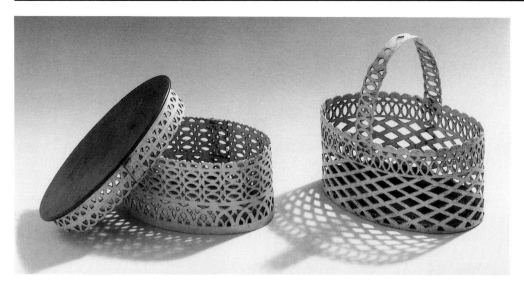

Whalebone box and basket

The sides of both these pieces are carved from single strips of curved bone attached to oval pine bases. Such items were given as gifts by whalemen to their sweethearts, and could well have been used as sewing boxes.

Whalebone and pine, English or American, late 19th century, each 25.5cm (10in) long

Whalebone and ivory swift

Used for winding yarn, or wool, the swift is both a practical and decorative example of the whaleman's craft. The central column and table clamp are made from turned and carved whale ivory decorated with inlaid baleen and mother-of-pearl. The lattice frame is made from whalebone and decorated with blue and yellow ribbon ties.

Whalebone and ivory, baleen and mother-of-pearl, English or American, late 19th century, 43cm (17in) high

nineteenth century and are decorated with famous shipping scenes and portraits.

Objects made from genuine whalebone and walrus ivory, whether antique or modern, are subject to many legal restrictions, and often require a license before being allowed to cross international borders. It is strongly recommended that professional advice is obtained before travelling with such a commodity.

Shell-work

The so-called sailors' valentines, made during the nineteenth century, are collages of coloured shells, arranged in geometric shapes, with mottos and verses. They are housed in double octagonal Spanish cedarwood cases, hinged together and covered with glass. They vary in size from about 8 to 15 inches in diameter, and the standard mottos used are 'Home Sweet Home', 'Forget Me Not' and 'When This You See, Remember Me'. They were originally thought to have been made by American and English sailors. However, it is currently thought that the craft originated in Barbados, as some valentines bear Barbadian retail labels and many of the shells used in the collages are indigenous to the West Indies. Ships from Great Britain, Holland and North America were regular visitors to Barbados during the nineteenth century, and such attractive items made obvious presents for those left at home.

Sailors' wool-work pictures and embroidery

Little is known about the sailor's skill with a needle and thread beyond such practical purposes as mending sails and patching clothes. That many seamen, however, were more than adept at sewing, is evident from the quality of some of the fine embroidery they produced. Working with multi-coloured silk threads to decorate sea bags and clothing, and with brightly dyed wools they produced wool-work ship portraits.

The best 'wool paintings' of named ships, marine views and flags are superb examples of the type of 'crewel work' which appears to have been popular in Great Britain throughout the nineteenth and early twentieth centuries. However, there are few documented examples of American origin and, therefore, when these do appear on the market, they can command high prices.

Prisoner-of-war work, 1795-1815

It is not surprising that there are many similarities between scrimshaw and the products of the Napoleonic prisoners-of-war. Both types of craftsmen had limited supplies of raw materials and tools, they were restricted by space, and had a disproportionate amount of time to devote to their craft. In addition, many of the French prisoners-of-war had served in naval ships and had, therefore, an understanding of the workings of a ship.

The basic raw materials available to prisoners in any great quantity were mutton and beef bones and these were whittled and carved into a plethora of domestic utensils, toys and models.

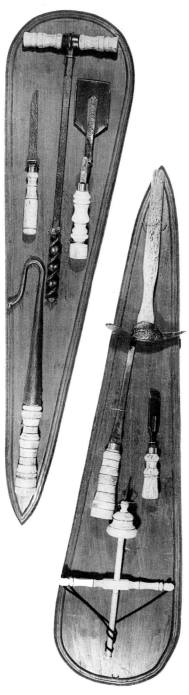

Part set of ship's carpenter's tools

Included are a hammer, a chisel, a hand-drill and a gouge, each with turned bone and ivory handles. The tools have been mounted on two display boards.

Whalebone and ivory, iron and pine, English, third quarter of the 19th century, 86cm (34in) high

Collection of shell valentines and souvenirs

This large assortment of items includes sewing boxes, needle cases and jewellery boxes, all of which are decorated with a variety of coloured shells. The shell-mounted frames enclose coloured prints of sailing ships, and the sailor's valentine from Barbados (bottom centre) is decorated with a heart and flower design incorporating the motto 'HOME AGAIN'.

Shell, wool and glass, 19th century, various sizes

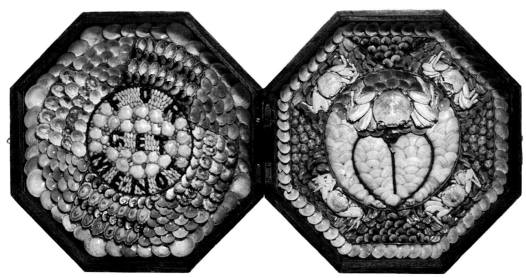

A pair of shell valentines

This collage of small coloured shells and small crab shells is mounted in a hinged pair of octagonal frames, and includes the motto 'FORGET ME NOT'. Such valentines were bought in the West Indies during the late 19th century, and brought back to Europe by travellers and sailors as presents for those left at home.

Shells, pine and glass, Jamaican, late 19th century, 23cm (9in) wide

Four sailors' valentines

The shell picture (top) is made from different coloured shells, mounted in an octagonal frame, with a central roundel containing a flower head and a heart. The wooden busk (bottom left) is inlaid with designs of hearts and flowers and is dated 1783. As it formed part of a lady's corset, it was a valentine that lay closest to her heart.

The other two items are a carved wood snuff box (bottom centre), in the shape of a fish, and a carved coconut shell (bottom right) inscribed 'When this you see, remember me, and bear me on your mind. Let all the world say what they will, speak of me as you find'.

Shell, mahogany, coconut, the shell picture 36cm (14in) wide

Needlework picture of *The Warriors of the Sea. A Lifeboat Story*

This unusual needlework picture narrates in verse the heroic rescue performed by the Lytham St Anne's lifeboat, and is mounted within an inlaid frame inset with portrait photographs of two members of the lifeboat crew and two illustrations of the monument erected in honour of those lost at sea.

Oak, wool and paper, English, c.1886, 93cm (36in) high

Oil and silk portrait of the schooner *Potency*

The background of this work is painted in oils but the hull, sails and rigging are constructed in relief with embroidered silk. Signed 'WILLIS N.Y.' and inscribed with the title 'POTENCY OF NATAL-BRAZIL CAPT. H. CHRISTENSEN'. The whole is mounted within its original moulded gesso frame.

Silk and oil, American, late 19th century, 48 x 70cm (19 x 28in)

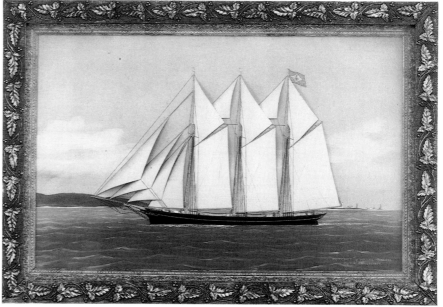

Wool and silk picture of
H.M.S. *Trafalgar*

This picture is unusual in the use of both wool and silk in its composition.

Silk and wood, English, late 19th century, 40 x 50cm (15¾ x 19¾in)

Wool picture

This picture contains an embroidered portrait of a ship-of-the-line in a central oval cartouche, framed by a border containing the flags of fourteen nations, a crown and drapes.

Wool, English, c.1860, 48 x 56cm (19 x 22in)

Prisoner-of-war bone-mounted games casket

The casket consists of a pine case with bone veneer and sliding arched lid. It is fitted with a set of double-nines dominoes, a set of miniature bone playing cards with painted court cards, a teetotum, counters and dice, and is inset with eight small watercolours of pastoral scenes and portraits. Gambling was a popular pastime for those in prison and games caskets were made and sold both to inmates and to those who attended local markets.

Bone and pine, French, early 19th century, 23cm (9in) long

Wool portrait of the frigate *Hercules*

This is a good example of a top-quality wool-work picture, showing the sailor's skilled use of colours and a distinctive stylized sea. Stitched 'T. Critchell HERCULES Feby 5th 1851'.

Wool, English, 1851, 57 x 73cm (22½ x 28¾in)

Collection of prisoner-of-war straw-work boxes and utensils

These domestic boxes, sold by Napoleonic prisoners-of-war at English markets to supplement their allowances, clearly indicate the levels to which the design and handling of coloured straw could be taken.

They include a face screen (far left), with a turned ivory handle, used to protect the face of a lady from the heat of the fire; four sewing boxes, each fitted with small compartments to house needles, wool, cotton and accessories; two boxes in the form of books (bottom right); a cigar case (far left); and a games box with a lid designed as a cribbage board (bottom right).

Pine, straw, ivory and glass, French, early 19th century, various sizes from 5cm (2in) long to 46cm (18in) long

As card games and gambling were the predominant pastimes of inmates, it is not surprising that many games compendiums were produced. These rectangular bone caskets incorporated a cribbage board, together with sets of dominoes and even miniature bone playing cards, with the suits painted in coloured inks. More appealing to the local ladies who purchased the prisoners' work in the markets adjacent to the prisons, were the bone-veneered sewing and jewellery boxes. A wooden casket, with hinged lid, was applied with decorative pierced-bone panels and backed with coloured paper, or tinfoil, to give an overall appearance of richness. Other household utensils made out of bone by prisoners included serving spoons, watch-cases, needle cases and tea caddies.

Bone models included small hand-cranked toys, called 'Spinning Jennies', with open construction showing gearing and with a handle at the front which, when turned, caused the figure of a lady, usually wearing a tall Breton hat, to move her head and arms while working on a spinning wheel. Sometimes the handle operated more than one figure and pieces were often coloured. Other more macabre models were the intricate model guillotines based on those used during the French Revolution. The platform supported a group of soldiers guarding a prisoner, whose neck lay on the guillotine block. When the blade was released, it dropped, neatly depositing the victim's head in an adjacent basket.

Straw-work is, perhaps, the most distinctive of all the prisoner handicrafts, with some examples displaying a level of craftsmanship which is quite outstanding. The craft was practised in France before the outbreak of hostilities, although the products tended to be rather mundane mats and small boxes. The basic method of decoration was to overlay, or inlay, a box or panel with strips of coloured straw arranged in a geometric pattern. Sometimes decorative pictures were created using coloured straw, and are most often found on the inside lid of work boxes. Another associated craft was the use of rolled and cut paper to decorate the lids and sides of tea caddies, or to create decorative landscapes or flower pictures, with watercolours and inks being used to embellish the composition.

Part of a sailor's duty on board ship was to make the lengths of rope, as supplied by the ropemaker, that were needed for the ship's standing-and-running rigging. This duty led to the derivation of the expression 'to know the ropes'. It required considerable skill, not only to separate the strands of a rope and to work and splice them successfully together, but also to create the many different knots, bends and hitches used for securing and joining pieces of rope, or making them fast to spars or other parts of the ship. Such intricate knots and splices were sometimes fashioned in small-scale and displayed on boards to exhibit the skill of a particular sailor, and to act as an attractive display of their craft. They were also often used as teaching aids for sea cadets.

Marine decorative arts

From the mid-eighteenth century, through to the recent Falklands conflict, British sailors and their gallant commanders have been held in great affection by the British public. There have also been, over the same period, astute entrepreneurs who, realizing their economic potential, have produced a wide range of commemorative wares and souvenirs celebrating naval victories. Some of these take the form of a piece of wood, a paperknife or a small barrel, to which a brass plaque

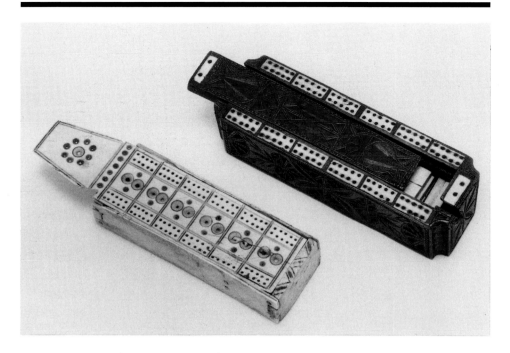

Two prisoner-of-war games caskets

The lower casket is constructed from pierced and carved bone, the other from oak. Both have a cribbage board design on the sliding lid and are fitted with set of bone dominoes.

Bone and oak, French, early 19th century, the larger 23cm (9in) long

Marquetry writing box

The lid of this walnut-veneered case is inlaid in coloured woods with two views of a schooner under sail. The inside is fitted with a writing slope, twin inkwells and a pen tray.

Walnut, rosewood, ebony and kingwood, English, early 20th century, 36cm (14in) wide

Collection of Nelson commemorative jugs and mugs

In creamware, prattware and pearlware, all these examples are decorated with transfers and hand-coloured.

Ceramic, English, 1800-20, various sizes

Collection of Staffordshire figures and groups

These pieces include a pair of the group 'Departure' and 'Return'.

Ceramic, English, 1810-30, various sizes

has been attached, purporting it to have been taken from the hull of one of the famous wooden men-of-war, such as the *Victory*, following the battle of Trafalgar. Also popular are the simple medals commemorating famous commanders and their achievements.

Much more plentiful are the ceramic wares produced throughout the eighteenth and nineteenth centuries and sold as relatively inexpensive, but highly decorative, domestic items. The earliest naval victories to be commemorated in this way, were the capture of Portobello, the Spanish port on the Isthmus of Darien, by Admiral Vernon with only six ships in 1739, and the seizing of the fort of San Lorenzo the following year. The delftware potteries in Lambeth, Bristol and Liverpool produced plates, bowls, mugs and jugs to commemorate these victories. They also started the trend, later most strongly developed by the Staffordshire potteries, of supplying the public with portrait figures, busts and medallions of the country's naval heroes. 'Toby' jugs, mugs, bowls and plates bearing patriotic mottoes were all produced in considerable numbers to commemorate famous naval commanders, as well as the colourful figure of 'Jack Tar' ashore and afloat.

During the 1760s, advances in the production of creamware, a refined cream-coloured earthenware dipped in liquid glaze, and the development of transfer-printing on earthenware by John Sadler of Liverpool, allowed potters to produce commemorative wares decorated with engravings after established artists. Many examples strongly reflected the enthusiasm of the public for a particular event, and today they have become documentary records of the period. Of these pieces, by far the greatest number relate to Horatio Nelson, commemorating his spectacular career and the battles in which he fought. Many were made between 1805 and 1806, when the country was mourning the death of its hero and celebrating his great victory at Trafalgar. However, there were at least six different Staffordshire groups depicting the death of Nelson produced throughout the 1840s. At the same time, a set of three standing figures were produced by the Staffordshire potteries depicting Nelson, the Duke of Wellington and Napoleon. Surprisingly, it was Napoleon who proved to be the best seller of the three, and he was later selected as the subject of the tallest, and finest, of all Staffordshire portrait figures, measuring 24 inches in height.

In addition to portraits of famous heroes, general figures of sailors were also made by the potteries over a period of some two hundred years, usually as part of a pair which included the sailor's sweetheart. Dressed in broad trousers and wearing typical three-cornered, or wide-brimmed, sailor hats, the later examples have titles such as 'The Shipwrecked Sailor'. Other groups are based on popular theatrical figures from performances such as 'The Pilot' and 'The Red Rover'.

The Sunderland potteries were famous for producing a series of inexpensive wares, known as 'gift china', which were particularly popular in the nineteenth century with sailors plying between the British ports. They included wall plaques with religious texts, frog mugs, puzzle jugs and bowls, decorated with freely-applied pink lustre and transfer designs of ships and sailors bidding their sweethearts goodbye, with mottoes and titles like 'The Sailor's Farewell', 'Jack on a Cruise' and 'The Sailor's Tear'. The pink lustre is distinguished by its speckled or blotted appearance, and although this effect was achieved by other potteries, all pieces of this genre are known as 'Sunderland'.

At first glance, the frog mug appeared like a typical transfer-decorated mug, until the drinker emptied the liquid contents and saw the realistic, full-size frog fixed to the inside base.

In some examples, the frog was hollowed out, so that it would spurt liquid into the face of the unsuspecting drinker.

Other gifts, popular in the mid-nineteenth century, included glass and earthenware rolling pins, treasured for their decorative qualities rather than for their practical culinary use. Decorated with either painted or transfer illustrations, they contained lettering referring to sailors, ships and the sea, as well as mottoes like 'Love and Be True', 'A Sailor's Gift' and 'Always Ready'. A large number of glass rolling pins were made in the Sunderland bottle glass factories, using the popular transfers which also appear on the lustre plaques and mugs made locally.

Another novelty, popular during the early eighteenth century, was the so-called puzzle jug. These vessels were made in a variety of earthenwares, including English delft, slipware, stoneware and creamware, and were applied with transfer designs depicting nautical and other subjects. The neck was decorated with pierced open-work, making the piece seemingly impossible to use. Although puzzle jugs varied greatly in style, the basic principle of design remained the same. The rim of the neck was mounted with a series of nozzles, which were connected to the interior of the jug by tubes running through the hollow handle. If all, but one, of the nozzles were covered by the user's fingers, then, in principle, it was possible to drink from the jug. However, the potter sometimes concealed a further nozzle to ensure the user was dowsed.

Presentation combined timepiece and aneroid barometer

The two dials are mounted within miniature ships' wheels and centred by crossed oars, an anchor and a life belt. The bevelled oak base has a presentation plaque engraved 'Presented to A. Mactavish By The Officers and Crew of H.M.S. Carabiner on the Occasion of his leaving the Steamer Tobermory 6th June 1898'.

Brass, oak, glass and steel, English, dated 1898, 44cm (17¼in) wide

Doulton Lambeth stoneware marine tyg

The three-handled mug, or 'tyg', is decorated with three panels containing portraits of sailing yachts. The whole is embellished with incised stylized fish and anchor designs.

Ceramic, English, c.1900, 20cm (8in) high

Majolica Isle of Man 'Union Jack' teapot and cover

This unusual vessel is modelled in the form of a three-legged sailor seated on a coiled rope, carrying a Union Jack in his left hand. The moulded mark on the base bears the inscription 'W Broughton 50 Duke St Douglas'.

Ceramic, Isle of Man, 1880s, 22cm (8¾in) high

Silver-gilt presentation box

The lid of the circular box is engraved with a scene of an engagement between French and English men-of-war. The base is engraved 'Captain Maitland on Board H.M.S. Bellerophon commemorating the surrender of Napoleon in his attempt to escape to the Americas in the year 1815'.

Silver, hall-marked London, 1795, 8.5cm (3¾in) diameter

Collection of jugs and mugs commemorating Lord Rodney

In creamware and Derby porcelain, these vessels celebrate Rodney's career, and specifically his victory over Admiral De Grass at the Battle of the Saints in 1782.

Ceramic, English, 1780-1800, various sizes

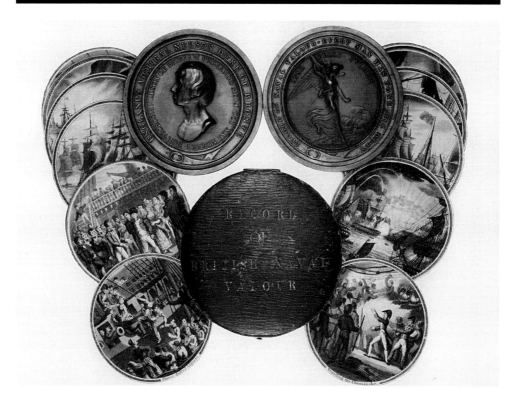

Naval bronze picture medal

The medal is cast in relief with a bust of Admiral Nelson and inscribed 'Record of Naval Valour Every Man Has Done His Duty'. The medal opens to reveal a compartment housing twelve coloured aquatints published by Edward Orme, after pictures by Jehoshaphat Aspins, entitled 'The Naval & Military Exploits which have distinguished the Reign of George the Third'. The whole medal is housed in a leather case.

Bronze, paper and leather, English, c.1820, 7.5cm (3in) diameter

Sailor-made watch-stand

This unusual carved oak stand has a central aperture for the insertion of a watch. The surround is carved in the form of two stylized fish.

Oak, English, third quarter of the 19th century, 45cm (17¾in) wide

Commemorative silver and enamel cigarette case

The lid is enamelled with a portrait of a steam yacht and other nautical motifs. The base is inscribed 'R.M.S. "Empress of China" (H.M. Armed Cruiser) Launched by Lady Northcote Barrow in Furness. 25th March 1891'.

Silver and enamel, hall-marked Chester, 1890, 8 x 11cm (3¼ x 4¼in)

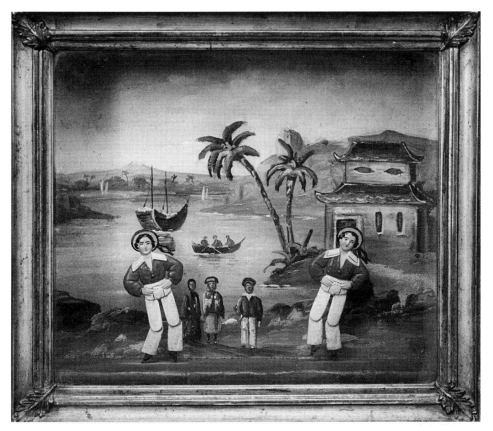

Lighthouse timepiece

The gilt-brass model of the lighthouse is fitted with a timepiece at the top of the revolving tower which is, in turn, powered by a clockwork movement housed in the base.

Brass and steel, English, early 20th century, 36cm (14in) high

Sailor's hornpipe automaton picture

The two articulated and painted metal figures of sailors dance a hornpipe to the tune of a small cylinder musical movement. The background is painted with a Far Eastern harbour scene, and the base contains the musical and clockwork automaton movement.

Tin, canvas and gilt gesso, English, late 19th century, 36 x 41cm (14 x 16in)

Ship Portrait Painting

THE CUSTOM of painting portraits of ships most probably originated with local amateur and professional house painters. With little or no formal training, they were commissioned to paint ship portraits for shipowners, visiting and resident Sea Captains and their crew. The practice thrived throughout Europe, North America and the Far East from the mid-eighteenth century, through to the early 1900s.

The quality of ship portraits varies from poor or mediocre, to those works with either true artistic merit, or naïve charm. They provide the marine historian with an important source of documentary information, since the name of the ship, the date and name of the owner, or Captain, is sometimes prominently written along the bottom of the painting. They are usually technically accurate, with correct outline, proportions and rigging, since any error would have been quickly identified by the trained eye of the buyer. Some portraits are painted with almost photographic accuracy which, combined with their two-dimensional quality, causes many to have a very flat and stiff appearance. Many paintings exhibit a strong use of colour and sometimes depict ships riding seas of uniform waves, with exaggerated billowing sails and outsize pennants bearing the ship's name. The patron, though possessing a trained technical eye, would normally have had only a limited appreciation of art, his points of artistic reference being no more than crude book illustrations and the carved and painted shop signs which decorated seaport towns.

On visiting a port, sailors would often buy, or commission, ship portraits with a background of the local harbour as a souvenir of their stay. Captains of merchant vessels would also commission portraits of their command, often showing the home port, to be hung with pride above the home hearth as mementoes for their families while they were away on long voyages. When a Captain received a new command it was not unusual for him to order a portrait of the ship, and this explains why several pictures of the same vessel often bear the names of different Captains on the plaque. Shipowners also commissioned portraits of ships in their fleet, which they then hung in the home port office to advertise the size and quality of individual vessels.

Techniques

Tommaso de Simone

BARQUENTINE JOHN WILLIAMSON, CAPT. YOUNG, LEAVING THE BAY OF NAPLES, 1871
Tommaso de Simone was one of a family of painters who lived and worked in Naples. The Bay of Naples was a favourite anchorage for yachts during the 19th century.

Oil on canvas, Italian, signed, inscribed with title and dated 1871, 51 x 76cm (20 x 30in)

By the end of the eighteenth century most of the ship portraits produced in north-western Europe were painted in oil on canvas. However, earlier portraits can sometimes be found painted on wood, often using the lid of a sailor's sea chest.

The votive pictures of the Iberian and Mediterranean ports were normally painted in either watercolour or gouache, an opaque form of watercolour which produced some of the richness of oils, but which could be applied to the paper in a much shorter period of time.

In Europe, the technique of painting on glass originated during the early years of the eighteenth century in Bohemia and Silesia, the traditional centres of the European glass industry. The trade later flourished in Augsburg, The Netherlands, France, Switzerland and England. However, by the mid-nineteenth century, the market for ship paintings on glass was dominated by a family of artists from Antwerp, called Weyts.

Owing to the complex process of painting on glass, many examples depict the simplest of designs and, sometimes, the most blatant of errors, such as the name of the ship spelt in reverse. The first stage of the process was for the artist to produce a pencil sketch of the vessel he intended to paint, although in the form of a reverse image to that of the completed glass picture. The drawing was then placed beneath a plate of glass, the upper surface of which was applied with a varnish. The artist then copied the drawing through the glass, the paint thus adhering to the varnished surface. In applying the paint, the secret was to start with the details in the foreground, as well as all lines and surfaces that were not crossed or concealed by other parts of the painting. These included the gilt decoration to the bow and stern, seams in the hull planking, rigging details, the sea's highlights in white and shadowing in black. The next step was to colour in the hull and outline the sails, subsequently adding the spars, masts and all rigging. At each stage the paint was allowed to dry, before finally the sea and sky were added to cover the whole area of the glass and the title of the ship was painted along the bottom of the picture, together, perhaps, with a date, the name of the Captain and the artist's signature.

It is the combination of the artist's great technical ability together with the unusual medium of a glass painting, which, no doubt, appealed to the nineteenth-century seaman, and which is still greatly prized today.

France and the Roux family of ship painters

It is primarily due to the work of one family of native Marseille marine painters, that this French port played such an important role in the history of ship portraiture during the heyday of sailing ships from the mid-eighteenth to the late nineteenth century. The family consisted of Joseph Roux (1725-93), his son, Antoine Roux (1765-1835), and three grandsons, Antoine (1790-1872), Frédéric (1805-70) and François (1811-82). The family ran a chandlery and chart-agent shop on the quayside of Marseille harbour, between Fort Saint-Jean and L'Hôtel de Ville. This location provided them with a wonderful view of the many ships moored in the harbour, and acted as an ideal gallery in which to display their art.

Portraits by Joseph Roux are relatively rare and can be distinguished from those of the later Roux painters by their more primitive style. Many of his subjects were influenced by contemporary wars at sea, and he became a competent recorder of naval engagements, particularly those which took place towards the end of his life.

The earliest known works by his son, Antoine, date from the 1780s, during which time the latter was producing votive paintings for local chapels and churches. Sketch books from this period show that, as a young man, Antoine drew sensitive and well-executed seascapes around the family home at Endoumer, near the town of Montandes. He later inherited his father's chandlery business and from here produced a prodigious number of good quality ship portraits. These were commissioned by Captains of all nationalities, although the lion's share went back to the New England ports on the east coast of America. Antoine signed his work 'Antoine Roux fils ainé' and was known as Antoine Roux père.

All three of Antoine's sons went on to work in the studio. The eldest, also called Antoine, signed his works 'Antoine Roux fils'. The second son, Frédéric, produced ship portraits and votive paintings in watercolour on paper and signed himself 'François Roux A Marseille', later moving to

Neopolitan School

The steamship *John H. Barry* in the Bay of Naples, and the steamship *John H. Barry* in stormy seas.
Typical of a pair of 'fair and foul' Neopolitan ship portraits, these works depict the 3083-ton steel screw steamer,
John H. Barry, in two contrasting seas. She was built in 1899 by J. L. Thompson of Sunderland for J. H. Barry
& Co of Whitby, and named after the owner.

Gouache, Italian, 40 x 66cm (15¾ x 26in)

Domenico Gavarrone

SHIP CAIRNGORM, CAPT. BOGLE. ENTERING THE PORT OF GENOA 1864
Domenico Gavarrone was an artist who lived and worked in Genoa. He appears to have graduated from painting primitive votive pictures, to producing competent ship portraits.

Watercolour and gouache heightened with scratching out, Italian, signed, inscribed with title and dated 1864, 45.5 x 70cm (18 x 27½in)

Honoré Pellegrini

BRIG ELEANOR GRACE OF SHIELDS, CAPT. J. ROBINSON, IN THE BAY OF MARSEILLES, 1851
Honoré Pellegrini was probably of Italian origin. He settled and worked in Marseille, where he was a contemporary of the Roux family.

Watercolour, pen and black ink, Italian, inscribed with title and dated 1851, 44 x 58cm (17¼ x 22¾in)

J., L. or E. Tudgay

The barque *Thomas Humphreys*.

Oil on canvas, English, signed and dated 1861, 52 x 77cm (20 x 30in)

Samuel Walters

The Baltimore clipper *Carrier Dove*.
The *Carrier Dove* was built by James Abraham of Baltimore in 1855. Later that year, she ran into a violent hurricane on her maiden voyage to Rio and lost her main-mast, as well as her fore and mizzen topmasts. She eventually continued on her voyage, docking in San Francisco on 25 April 1856.

Oil on canvas, English, signed and dated, 74 x 112cm (29 x 44in)

Le Havre. Finally, the youngest son, François, started painting at an early age, and in later life, produced many carefully detailed views of the French iron-clads and battle fleet.

The prolific output of the Roux studio overshadowed work being produced in other French ports such as Brest, Cherbourg, Dunkirk and Le Havre. The Roux portraits may not be considered great works of art, and yet the combination of well-detailed and accurately rendered vessels, together with the competent treatment of sea, sky and background, means that these portraits have consistently appealed to collectors over the centuries.

The Mediterranean painters

It became almost obligatory for a north European Captain, visiting one of the many Mediterranean ports on a maiden voyage, to return home with a portrait of his command. In addition to the Roux family of Marseille, there was a strong tradition of ship portraiture in Genoa, Leghorn and Naples, while on Italy's Adriatic coast the principal centres of production were in Venice, Ancona and Trieste.

Italian portraits, painted in a combination of watercolours and ink, were carefully detailed and often depicted lively scenes. They were frequently produced as pairs of 'fair weather-foul weather' portraits. The Bay of Naples was a favourite setting, with Mount Vesuvius smoking in the background and the vessel either under full sail, or at anchor in calm waters. The companion picture illustrated a very different scene, with the same vessel battling through heavy seas with furled and tattered sails, and sometimes dismasted or otherwise disabled.

English Primitive School

THE FLEET OFF SHORE –
A REVIEW AT SPITHEAD
A charming panorama of the fleet flying outsize flags and lying at anchor off Spithead. The foreground depicts couples strolling along the beach, a person of importance being conveyed in a carriage, and sailors smoking clay pipes and arranging provisions for the ships.

Oil on panel, English, c.1785, 42 x 165cm (16½ x 65in)

Throughout the nineteenth century, Valetta, on the island of Malta, was a favourite anchorage for large cruising yachts and, more importantly, served as the base for the Royal Navy's extensive Mediterranean fleet. For this reason, the harbour appears in the background of many ship portraits.

British ports

London

As the world's leading seafaring nation, Great Britain provided a huge and profitable market for the sale and production of ship portraits throughout the eighteenth and nineteenth centuries. William John Huggins (1781-1845) was an accomplished marine artist and, although not strictly falling into the category of 'pierhead painter', he was extremely popular among seafarers, directly influencing a new generation of marine painters. His output was considerable, and ship portraits formed only part of a much larger production of marine paintings, which included both naval engagements and sea pageants. Serving in the East India Company until 1814, Huggins subsequently set up as an artist in London, where he was joined by his son-in-law, Edward Duncan, who produced inexpensive engravings of his work, thus exposing it to a much wider audience.

The Tudgay family are recorded as being ship painters in London during the third quarter of the nineteenth century. Although little is known about their history, it is thought that F. Tudgay worked as a cabin painter for the shipbuilder, Richard Green, at his yard at Blackwall on the

Thames. Works by J., L., and E. Tudgay are recorded, and their paintings, normally executed in oils, are honest and accurate, rather than inspired.

Liverpool

The thriving port of Liverpool was one of the prime sources of ship paintings for the English and American markets. The principal marine painter of the city was Samuel Walters (1811-82). He accepted many commissions for ship portraits and, as steamships became more common, was equally successful in producing paintings of both steam and sailing ships.

William Howard Yorke (fl.1865-1913), although a member of the Liverpool school of ship portraitists, was rather less academic in the approach to his work than some of his contemporaries. His father was also a ship painter, and it is probable that the earlier style of ship paintings, simply signed 'Yorke', are by him rather than by William.

Hull and the east coast ports

An interesting school of marine painters, led by John Ward (1798-1849), originated in Hull. Ward was apprenticed to a house and ship painter, worked as a sign-writer and had first-hand experience of life at sea aboard an Arctic Hull whaler. Ward was an excellent draughtsman and lithographer, producing a number of instruction books for sign-writers and lithographs of shipping scenes, intended for aspiring marine artists. Another member of the Hull school was Thomas Binks (1799-1852), who produced cheerful paintings in bright-coloured oils. In addition to standard ship portraits, his work also included whalers and the newly introduced paddle-steamers.

Other members of the Hull school included J. Fannen (fl.1880-1910), who worked in oils and portrayed a variety of sailing vessels, including coasters and colliers from British, Scandinavian and Dutch ports. His backgrounds often included topographical views of the coastline around Tynemouth and Flamborough Head. Reuben Chappell (1870-1940), was another artist who began his career as a ship portraitist on the river Humber. Chappell was apprenticed to a local photographer where he was employed to tint images, and it is possibly here that he learnt the rudiments of painting. He augmented his modest income by submitting line drawings to the local paper, and by the time he reached his twenties, he had his own studio and advertised himself as a photographer and artist.

Chappell initially produced work for the masters of sloops and other river craft that travelled up the Humber estuary. As they received only modest incomes, and were thus unable to afford expensive oil portraits, so Chappell changed to the more traditional British medium of watercolour, which allowed him to produce paintings quickly and more cheaply. In 1904, he moved to Par in Cornwall on account of poor health. Here he continued to earn a living painting the ketches, schooners and small steamers that visited the harbour from the nearby ports of Charlestown and Fowey, often producing pairs of 'fair weather-foul weather' paintings, similar in style to the Italian artists. His backgrounds generally incorporated famous local sights, such as the Lizard headland and the lighthouses at Eddystone and Spurn Head.

Chappell's work is well documented, and it appears he averaged some 300 paintings a year. Each work listed the name of the vessel, the port of registration and often the name of the master.

Harold Percival

A portrait of the windjammer *Mermerus* of Greenock. Percival was one of the more skilful ship portrait painters working in Liverpool during the last quarter of the 19th century. He specialized in portraying windjammers in heavy seas and normally signed his paintings 'H. Percival' in ink.

Watercolour, heightened with white, English, end of the 19th century, 12.5 x 19cm (5 x 7½in)

W. T. Liley

A primitive portrait of the cross-channel paddle-steamer, *City of London*, leaving Dover with a full passenger deck and a strong following wind.

Oil on canvas, English, 19th century, signed, 46 x 61cm (18 x 24in)

MENAI OF LONDON.

P. N.

The cutter *Menai of London*.
The cutter is shown sailing off Cowes, and is flying the Royal Yacht Club pennant.

Oil on glass, Belgian, inscribed with title and initialled 'P. N.', 35 x 50cm (11¾x 19in)

English School

The White Star liner *Adriatic* passing Bishop's Rock.
The *Adriatic* was launched in 1872 and quickly built up a reputation for fast Atlantic crossings. Her second voyage to New York established a new record for the first westward crossing of the Atlantic in under eight days. After the completion of the *Germanic* in 1875, the *Adriatic* was chartered to the Occidental & Oriental Line for their new San Francisco to China route.

Oil on canvas, English, 19th century, 51 x 81cm (20 x 32in)

He rarely dated his works, still signing himself 'R. Chappell, Goole', even after his move to Cornwall. Later paintings, however, were signed 'R. Chappell' and sometimes simply 'R. C.'

Bristol

The only artist of note to emerge from Bristol, the fourth great port of England, was Joseph Walters (1783-1856), who lived and worked in the city all his life. Although more commonly known as a general marine artist, he could also produce fine ship portraits when commissioned to do so by an owner or Captain.

Belgium

From the 1830s until approximately 1878, Antwerp was renowned as the centre for painting on glass, with the Weyts family its chief exponents. The originator of this specialist art form was Wenzeslaus Wieden (1769-1814), from the Belgian port of Ostend. He was followed by Petrus Weyts (1799-1855), who, with his four sons, produced large numbers of ship paintings on glass.

P. N.

H.M.S. CASTOR RUNNING DOWN THE CAMELEON CUTTER OFF DOVER AUGT. 27 1834
Although there are many known glass paintings bearing the initials 'P. N.', the artist has not, as yet, been identified. However, it is known that he was a contemporary of Petrus Weyts, and many of the vessels depicted in his works are connected with Ostend.

Oil on glass, Belgian, inscribed with title and dated 1834, 42 x 61cm (16½ x 24in)

All four members of the Weyts family are described in the local register as artists, although it appears that the majority of work was actually produced by Petrus, as up until his death, all surviving examples are signed solely by him. His style varied considerably, with ships portrayed both under full sail and with reduced canvas. Some portraits depict ships sailing on the port tack, with sails seen from the front, and others on the starboard tack, with sails seen from the stern and all rigging visible. He followed tradition, and was meticulous where the protocol of painting flags' and pennants was concerned. These included the name of the vessel painted on a pennant flying from the mainmast, the national flag of the port of registration and sometimes an identification code number spelt out in four flags. The rigging was always shown in great detail and the hull shape accurately portrayed, in order that the ship could be readily identified. It was traditional to depict the deck with several sailors in flat-topped headgear, while the Captain was sometimes shown giving orders with an outstretched arm. The background often contained several vessels, one a repeat of the subject vessel seen from a different angle, the other usually a pilot cutter. Normally a port was pictured in the background, sometimes Ostend or, more often, Flushing. Petrus Weyts always added a descriptive text to his paintings, detailing the type of ship, her name and port of registration, the name of the Captain and sometimes the place where the ship was portrayed.

With the death of Petrus Weyts in 1855, his son Carolus took charge of the workshop. A distinctive change in the style of painting can be seen from this date, with seas and skies handled in a less stylized manner. Unfortunately, Carolus's early death in 1875 virtually brought to an end the tradition of glass-painting in Antwerp.

Alexander Lamartinière

A glass painting of the cutter *Albert-Louise D'honfleur*. Alexander Lamartinière (fl.1840–65) was probably of Flemish origin, and was one of the few glass painters who pursued this style of painting outside Flanders.

Oil on glass with gouache, Flemish, inscribed with title and dated 1851, 46 x 59cm (18 x 23½in)

Weyts family

*ANNE OF GOOLE, SAMUEL HALL,
MASTER. PASSING OSTEND, 1854*
Petrus Weyts, who lived and
worked in Antwerp, was renowned
for his portraits of ships painted on
glass. With the help of his brother,
Ignatius, he established a studio,
where he was also helped by his
son, Carolus, and between them
they produced many glass
paintings for the shipping trade
operating out of the busy port of
Antwerp.

*Oil on glass, Belgian, inscribed
with title and dated 1854,
56 x 72cm (22 x 28¼in)*

The Netherlands

Holland, one of the greatest of the world's early seafaring nations, was home for many of the 'old
masters' of marine painting. However, during the nineteenth century, there were only a very
limited number of artists in Holland who specialized in ship portraiture alone.

In addition to the larger sea-going vessels operating out of the ports of Amsterdam and
Rotterdam, the wide range of coastal vessels and barges plying the country's canals provided a
wealth of inspiration for the marine artist. Jacob Spin (1806-75), lived and worked in Amsterdam,
and it was from here that he produced accomplished ship portraits in watercolour. It is thought
that he trained as a draughtsman, during which time he acquired his skills as a watercolourist.
Another Dutch marine artist, D. A. Teupken (1828-59), painted a number of the smaller vessels
that traded between the east coast of Britain and Amsterdam. His father, D. A. Teupken (1801-
45), was also a portrait painter in watercolours, although his style was more naïve and he signed
his work 'D. A. Töpke'.

Rotterdam, being better placed as an international sea port, benefitted from the increase in
trade during the latter half of the nineteenth century. P. Vermaas worked here between 1865 and
the early years of this century, producing oil paintings of the many steam and sailing ships that
called at the port.

Germany

The German province of Schleswig-Holstein contained several seaports, all of which had belonged to Denmark prior to 1864. The province supported a prosperous merchant navy and a number of talented artists, whose work was known locally as 'captains' pictures'. They tended to live in Altona, and found inspiration and contacts at the nearby international port of Hamburg.

During the first half of the nineteenth century, there were a number of artists in Germany with the name Hansen. They produced paintings of local North Sea traders, English colliers and Welsh schooners carrying slate to the growing city of Hamburg. B. B. Hansen (fl. 1827-60), H. C. Hansen and J. Hansen are all recorded as having produced work during this period.

The construction of the port of Bremerhaven in 1827, stimulated shipping to use the river Weser, and thus created further demand for portraits. The foremost artist in the Bremerhaven area was Carl J. H. Fedler (1799-1858), who settled in the town of Bremen in 1831. He produced a number of works in oil and published a series of lithographs depicting local ships. One of the most prolific painters during this time was Ottomann Jaburg (1830-1908), who, in spite of the often poor quality of his output, was one of the most popular painters of his generation. Many examples of his work are still extant today.

Scandinavia

Whilst a small number of ship portraits were painted in Denmark around the middle of the eighteenth century, it was not until the early nineteenth century that such paintings were produced in any great numbers. The leading Danish painter, Jacob Petersen (1774-1855), was born in Flensburg. He joined the Danish Navy and later rose to the rank of Captain. Following his retirement from the Navy, he produced many portraits of English and American ships, usually with Kronberg castle in the background. He normally worked in watercolours or gouache and, despite having received some tuition at the Copenhagen Academy of Art, his work displays a primitive quality.

America

Throughout the nineteenth century, the New England ports of America were the scene of a thriving ship portrait industry, whose products were similar in style to those of the European schools. Many early examples of American work depict vessels from two different angles: the full broadside and a smaller, usually stern-on view. Two types of ship portraits are unique to America: those of the famous Baltimore clipper ships, and those depicting the various aspects of the American whaling trade.

The most famous American painter of steamships was, in fact, the Danish artist, Antonio Jacobsen. Born into a family of Copenhagen violin makers, Jacobsen emigrated to New York in 1871 at the age of twenty-one, having benefitted from an academic training in art. He initially found employment with a safe manufacturer, where he painted marine views on to the doors of safes purchased by shipping lines. This decoration was noticed by an employee of the old

Dominion Line, who subsequently encouraged Jacobsen to take up ship portraiture as a profession. At first, Jacobsen painted New York sailing packets and schooners. However, he made his reputation with the steam and sail portraits he painted in considerable numbers for the famous shipping lines of the day. He was fortunate enough to find himself working during the height of the competition between the shipping companies operating on both sides of the Atlantic, all of whom required promotional paintings of their fleets in an effort to attract the travelling public to use their ships.

In the specialist field of American river and lake steamers, the portrait market was dominated by the twin brothers, James and John Bard, who worked in the countryside around the Hudson River. They signed their early works 'J. & J. Bard'. However, after John's death in 1856 the surviving brother signed himself 'James Bard', together with his address, as a means of advertising his works.

The Far East

Chinese artists developed a technique for painting highly detailed portraits, using oils on linen. The earliest examples date from the 1830s, although it was not until the middle of the nineteenth century, and the arrival of the great tea clippers in large numbers, that the Chinese ship portrait industry began to flourish. Examples of Chinese work, usually by anonymous artists, are recorded as having been produced in Calcutta and Bombay, as well as in the ports of Foochow, Macao and Hong Kong. In general, the earlier paintings were somewhat lacking in style and dramatic effect. They virtually all depicted the traditional profile view until the latter part of the nineteenth century when, under the influence of European styles, several artists, most notably Lai Fong of Calcutta (fl. 1890-1910), started producing portraits of big square riggers, which were almost indistinguishable from their European counterparts.

The ships

The Baltimore clippers

The title 'clipper' ship, is the name given to a vessel that was constructed for speed. The term was first used to describe the fast schooners built in Virginia and Maryland, known as Baltimore clippers, and which became famous during the 1812 War as blockade runners and privateers. The hull design was long and sleek, with a draught deeper aft than forward. The hull was sharply inclined, bow and stern, thus reducing the area of the hull in contact with the water. The masts were extensively raked and the most popular rig was that of a schooner with square topsails on one or both masts.

Today, portraits of Baltimore clippers are much sought-after, as few were produced, and they appeal, in particular, to the American collector due to their romantic involvement in the early history of the United States. The true Baltimore clippers were a short-lived breed of ship and, as far as the general public is concerned, the term 'clipper' has become synonymous with the graceful full-rigged vessels of the mid-nineteenth century, once the fastest ships in the world.

The later American clippers

The discovery of gold in California in 1848, and later in Australia in 1850, together with the relaxing of the British Navigation Act in 1849, resulted in a pressing demand for larger and faster passenger and freight carrying vessels. This demand was initially taken up by the Boston shipbuilder, Donald McKay, who produced many of the so-called fine clippers, including the *Sovereign of the Seas*, built in 1852, which was chartered by James Baines for his Black Ball Line. She was used on the lucrative Australian routes, and set a new record of sixty-five days for the Liverpool to Melbourne run, which remained unbroken for the next thirty years.

James Butterworth (1768-1842) and his son, James Edward Butterworth (1817-94), emigrated to America from Liverpool in the 1840s and set up a studio near New York, specializing in the painting of clippers, including the largest ever constructed, the *Great Republic*. Built on the east coast of America, and launched throughout the 1850s and 60s, these powerful wooden ships were capable of carrying prospectors around Cape Horn to the goldfields of California. They were also used to transport emigrants to Australia and bring back tea from the Far East, where they were portrayed by Chinese painters operating in the tea-loading ports of Shanghai and Hong Kong. Artists included Chong Qua, in Hong Kong, and Chow Kwa, in Shanghai.

The British clippers

In contrast to the American clippers, the British clippers were initially smaller in size. Nevertheless, with the growth of the transatlantic and Far East trade during the middle years of the nineteenth century, British shipbuilders were encouraged to produce a number of fine vessels.

Following the financial depression of 1857 and the Civil War of 1861-65, America experienced a decline in shipbuilding, which resulted in the expansion of Britain's fleet of famous tea clippers. Since the first crop of tea to arrive in London each season would command a huge premium, it was of paramount importance for owners to have the fastest available ships in their fleets. Clippers were regularly involved in highly competitive races from China to London, with contestants often arriving within hours of each other after a journey of some 16,000 miles, as happened after the legendary dash home in 1866. F. Tudgay (fl. 1860) produced one of the only surviving paintings of the most famous tea clipper, the *Cutty Sark*, in her original rig, and this proved to be of great importance when the ship was re-rigged in dry dock in 1957.

One of the most prolific ship portraitists was Thomas Dutton (1819-91), who, in spite of painting a wide range of sailing vessels, is probably best known today for his pictorial records of tea clippers. Working in watercolour, he produced fine quality lithographs which were subsequently published by Ackermann.

The windjammers

A popular, non-nautical, term by which square-rigged sailing ships from the last quarter of the nineteenth century were often referred to, is 'windjammer'. In comparison to the four-masted barque or windjammer, the clippers were built for speed. However, they were expensive to construct and maintain, due to the punishment experienced by sailing at high speeds, often over

John Henry Mohrmann

A portrait of the barque *Kilmeny*. John Mohrmann was born in San Francisco and went to sea at the early age of thirteen. He worked initially as a picture restorer in England before settling in Antwerp in 1890, where he established a studio for ship portraiture. His output was prolific, and he often painted large scale views of vessels, paying great attention to details such as deck fittings and rigging.

Oil on canvas, American, 1890s, signed, 60 x 90cm (23½ x 39in)

Lai Fong of Calcutta

The iron four-masted barque *Trafalgar*.
The *Trafalgar* was built in 1877 by C. Connell & Co. of Glasgow for A. Brown & Co. She was bought by A. Weir & Co. in 1893; the company flag can be seen in this painting.

Oil on canvas, Chinese, signed, inscribed and dated Calcutta 1889, 55 x 84cm (23 x 33in)

15 knots, with some vessels even attaining 20 knots or more. Clippers also required a crew of up to 100 men and boys, in contrast to the windjammer, which could carry twice the cargo with, perhaps, a crew of only twenty-five. Such cargo vessels, however, could not compete visually with the sleek lines and massive sail area of the clippers, and they also lacked the carved trail boards at the bow and gilt decoration at the stern. The windjammer had a wall-sided hull and an almost square mid-ship section, allowing for maximum cargo capacity. The masts were relatively short compared with the length of the hull and rigged with long spars and narrow square sails.

The American schooners

The traditional schooner was a small, two-masted vessel which carried fore-and-aft sails and whose main mast was taller than its fore mast. However, three-, four- and five-masted schooners were quite common, and there was even one celebrated seven-master, the *Thomas W. Lawson*. They were largely used for the coastal trade in coal and ice off North America and for fishing on the Grand Banks off Newfoundland. The larger schooners, with up to six masts, could be handled by a reduced crew of between twelve and fifteen hands, with the help of steam donkey-engines to work the windlass, hoist the sails and operate the pumps and other essential equipment. These craft were used for trading well into the twentieth century, when they were finally replaced by coastal steamers.

One of the most eminent painters of the multi-masted schooners was William Pierce Stubbs of New England. He painted exclusively in oils, and depicted broadside views of these vessels, normally under full sail.

The steamers

The first regular steam passenger service to operate in European waters began on the Clyde in 1812, with the steam paddle-boat *Comet* servicing the ports of Greenock and Helensburgh. However, in America, Robert Fulton's *Clermont* started service on the Hudson River between New York and Albany in 1807. The following year another paddle-steamer, the *Phoenix*, was built to work on the Delaware River. However, as she initially had to travel from New York to Philadelphia, she became the first sea-going steamship. In 1819, the *Savannah* was the first steamship to cross the Atlantic, however, her claim to fame is tenuous since, although she was a fully rigged ship with steam engine, she had collapsible paddle-wheels which were used only sparingly during the crossing.

The first propeller-driven vessel to cross the Atlantic was the *Great Britain*, designed by Isambard Kingdom Brunel and launched in 1843. She had an all-iron hull, and despite being able to reach speeds of 9 knots, passengers had yet to completely trust the steam engine and, therefore, in common with other early steamships, she was fitted with sails on all six of her masts. It was not until the 1890s that auxiliary sails were finally abandoned on steamers, the yards removed and the masts shortened.

By far the most prolific artist specializing in steamships was the Danish artist, Antonio Jacobsen (1850-1921), who, it is claimed, kept a stock of canvases, apparently pre-painted by his wife and daughter with seas and skies, to which he added the appropriate steamer as orders were placed.

By the end of the nineteenth century, the tradition of ship portrait painting had radically declined, coinciding with the disappearance of large sailing vessels from ports around the world. The camera had already begun to capture much of this market and, coupled with the advancement of technology, ships spent much less time in port, thereby allowing only a very limited period for the artist to generate or execute much business. Sadly, although photography recorded the changing designs of shipbuilding during the twentieth century, the naïve charm of the portraits of pierhead painters was to be lost.

Beken & Son

The racing schooner *Margherita*. For over 100 years, the Beken family have been the most prominent photographers of private yachts and merchant shipping on the Solent. Frank Beken's photographs caught the golden age of yachting when European royal familes, including Czar Nicholas, Queen Victoria and the German Kaiser, spent several weeks on board their splendid yachts off Cowes.

Photographic silver print, English, 1913, 28 x 23cm (11 x 9in)

Ocean Liner Artefacts and Ephemera

THE TERM 'Ocean Liner' refers to any ship which belonged to a company providing scheduled ocean routes to fare-paying passengers. The heyday of the business began with the introduction of the steam turbine in the late nineteenth century, and lasted until air travel became the predominant form of international transport following World War II.

The most famous steamship line was Cunard, founded in 1840 by Samuel Cunard of Halifax, Nova Scotia, in partnership with George Burns. The first liners to offer a regular transatlantic passenger and mail service were wooden paddle-steamers. However, as the transatlantic trade developed, particularly with the advent of steel construction, Cunard increased both the size and number of its ships, in order to maintain its position as market leader.

In 1907, Cunard launched the liner, *Lusitania*. At 30,396 gross tons, she was the world's largest vessel, with accommodation for 552 first-, 460 second- and 1,186 third-class passengers. The first-class public rooms and private suites were furnished with carved mahogany panelling, impressive glass chandeliers and the most luxurious furnishings available during the Edwardian era. Together with her sister ship, *Mauretania*, she was a supreme example of the shipbuilder's and fitter's art. Her electric generating plant provided a 'new' form of power for several passenger lifts, refrigeration units, heating plants, ventilation fans, galley equipment and many other services. She captured the prestigious 'Blue Riband', a notional trophy for the fastest crossing of the Atlantic, from the Norddeutscher Lloyd's *Kaiser Wilhelm II* in 1907, by crossing at an average speed of 23.99 knots.

The other great pre-war Cunard liner was the *Aquitania*, with a displacement of 45,647 tons. Delivered in 1914, she completed three transatlantic round voyages before the outbreak of World War I. She provided superb first-class accommodation, and proved to be one of the longest serving liners, finally being broken up in 1950.

At the same time, both the White Star Line and the Hamburg-Amerika Line were building luxury liners capable of making the Atlantic crossing at moderate speeds. The quality of speed and accommodation changed, however, when the giant *Olympic* of 45,324 tons was delivered by Harland & Woolf to the White Star Line in 1911. She had accommodation for 689 first-, 674 second- and 1,026 third-class passengers. In addition to the magnificent public rooms, the first-class passengers could avail themselves of such facilities as a swimming-pool, Turkish baths and squash courts.

The *Olympic* was the first of an intended trio of ships to be built for the White Star Line's prestigious Southampton to New York service. Her sister ship, *Titanic*, struck an iceberg on her maiden voyage, with the loss of 1,490 lives. She was built to strict safety regulations and was considered, at the time, to be virtually unsinkable, having sixteen water-tight compartments. The disaster led to new regulations, which required that sufficient lifeboats be available for all passengers, and a more southerly route to be taken across the Atlantic. There is a somewhat morbid fascination with this sad event, and any material such as newspaper cuttings, copies of

F. Simpson

ORIENT CO.'S PLEASURE CRUISE BY THE S.S. 'LUSITANIA' TO THE WEST INDIA ISLANDS, MADEIRA, TENERIFFE, AZORES, &C. FROM LONDON

Chromolithographic poster, English, 102 x 76cm (40 x 30in)

telegrams or any other commemorative wares, can command high prices. The third liner, the *Britannic*, was completed in 1915 for service as a hospital ship during World War I, but was sunk by a mine later that year.

In 1915, in a bid to modernize its fleet, the Union Castle Mail Steamship Co., which ran a weekly service to Cape Town, placed an order for the 18,980 ton *Arundel Castle*, eventually launched in 1919. She was a coal-burning steamship of old-fashioned design, with four thin funnels, the aft one being a dummy. Another company who still preferred the steam-powered ships rather than those with oil-fired engines, was the Peninsular & Orient (P. & O.), who had large fleets operating east of Suez and needed a service of maximum reliability.

By the late 1920s, with the influence of the depression, combined with restrictive immigration policies and fierce competition between shipping companies, radical changes were developing in the passenger class structure. Maintaining the first-class as an élite service, the second- and third-classes were amalgamated to form a 'tourist-class', which eventually displaced all other secondary grades, apart from steerage accommodation.

The German line, Norddeutscher Lloyd, recaptured the Blue Riband in 1929 and, in a bid to retain supremacy on the profitable North Atlantic route, launched the new 51,656 ton *Bremen*, together with her sister ship, *Europa*. Both were fitted with an aircraft catapult and a Heinkel plane, enabling mail to be delivered to the next port of call whilst the ship itself was still some 600 miles from port.

To counteract this aggressive German competition, Cunard placed an order in May 1930, with John Brown & Co. of Clydebank, for the construction of an impressive and fast liner to replace the ageing fleet of *Mauretania*, *Aquitania* and *Berengaria* (*ex Imperator*). Finally launched in 1934, after a delay of two years due to the world-wide recession, the *Queen Mary* was the largest and fastest luxury liner afloat, providing accommodation for 776 first-, 784 tourist- and 579 third-class passengers. Although the *Queen Mary* had few new innovations, during her thirty-one years of service, both as a passenger liner and troop-carrier, she built up a loyal following and became a symbol of national greatness.

The French also joined the battle for supremacy on the North Atlantic routes with the building of the stylish 1,029 foot *Normandie*. Launched in 1932, she took two years to fit out and displayed the clean lines of the French design of the period. She had streamlined funnels and a sumptuous interior, with large public rooms decorated in the art deco style, a 100-foot long swimming pool, a theatre salon with fully-equipped stage and bridge rooms, a chapel, smoking rooms and several bars. The main stairway was constructed from marble, with a large bronze allegorical figure symbolizing Normandy mounted at the crest. She was certainly considered one of the most chic liners of the 1930s, and won the Atlantic Blue Riband on her maiden voyage in 1935.

Throughout the golden period of ocean travel, many passengers collected souvenirs of their voyage. These often included menus of the lavish meals enjoyed on board ship, and which were occasionally signed by fellow guests and officers of the shipping company. A great deal of printed material was issued by the shipping lines, including daily newspapers, itineraries and programmes of daily events, games and competition literature, lecture notes and brochures. Such mementoes can be found today in second-hand book shops, or with dealers of printed ephemera. Furthermore, all the larger shipping companies advertised their fleets and services by printing and distributing lithographic posters. Norman Wilkinson worked for Cunard, Austin Cooper for

Royal Mail and Frank Newbold for Orient Lines. In France, A. M. Cassandre designed some extremely stylish posters for the French Line.

Interior fixtures and fittings from liners were occasionally used for fitting-out hotels and offices, although few pieces appear on the market today. The traditional teak folding deckchairs can sometimes be found, although many replicas are now being produced. Many lines produced tableware either applied with company transfers, or impressed with the company motif, and these items can occasionally be found in small numbers today.

Anon

CUNARD LINE TO ALL PARTS OF THE WORLD

Chromolithographic poster showing a section of the Lusitania, *English, 102 x 76cm (40 x 30in)*

Anon

CUNARD EUROPE – AMERICA

Chromolithographic poster, English, 102 x 76cm (40 x 30in)

Anon

An invitation to the launching of the Cunard liner S.S. *Mauretania*.

Hand-coloured print, English, 25 x 20cm (10 x 8in)

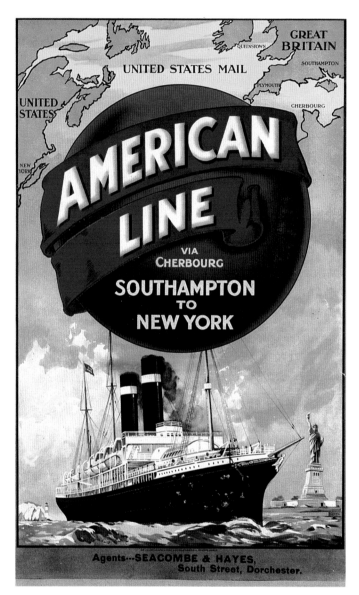

James S. Mann

ALLAN LINE ROYAL MAIL TO AND FROM CANADA

Chromolithographic poster, English, 102 x 76cm (40 x 30in)

Anon

AMERICAN LINE VIA CHERBOURG SOUTHAMPTON TO NEW YORK

Chromolithographic poster, American, 102 x 76cm (40 x 30in)

Montague B. Black

WHITE STAR LINE EUROPE TO AMERICA

Chromolithographic poster, English, 102 x 76cm (40 x 30in)

Odin Rosenvinge

CUNARD EUROPE AMERICA

Chromolithographic poster of the Berengaria, *English, 102 x 76cm (40 x 30in)*

Caring for Marine Collectables

OWNING a decorative work of art can be both a pleasure and, sometimes, quite a responsibility. Understanding the effects of the atmosphere on a wide range of material such as ivory, paper, cloth and wood, and knowing how to compensate for these, is an important part of caring for such items. Some superficial cleaning may be done using the simplest methods and materials and this will not only enhance the appearance of the object, but might well negate the need for expensive conservation at a later date. However, unless many precautions are taken, there may well be an occasion when professional conservation or restoration proves necessary.

Ivory and bone

The greatest threat to objects made from ivory and bone is that of drying out, which results in surface cracking. In order to remain in peak condition, with a good-quality sheen, pieces of bone and ivory should be treated with an oil. Pure lanolin is the best substance, although almond oil can also be used, but it will give a slight colour to the surface. Pure lanolin can be purchased from a local pharmacy. It should be applied sparingly and left on the surface for between five minutes and half an hour, depending on the extent of the dryness, and then gently polished off.

Both teeth and bone deteriorate in a dry atmosphere and large collections should be housed in a humidified case. One or two examples can, however, be protected by placing a glass of water, draped in muslin, in the display case. This should be checked on a regular basis in order that the water level is not allowed to drop below that of the muslin. The relative humidity should remain at a constant 50-55 per cent.

Ivory and bone should never be left in direct sunlight, as the radiation will discolour the surface and hasten the drying out process. Furthermore, pieces should not be left resting on strongly coloured or dyed fabrics or on varnished woods, as prolonged contact, combined with light, can tint the surface a similar colour to the background.

Ship models

Ship models, made from a diversity of materials such as ivory, bone, wood, thread, brass and horn, are always susceptible to changes in temperature and humidity. An uncased model also attracts household dust and grime which, over the years, can build into a thick coating and is often difficult to remove. Superficial dust can be removed by the careful application of an air spray, however, any further cleaning should be done by a professional restorer. The making of a glazed display case to house a ship model will deter further soiling, and an atmospheric drying agent should be incorporated to ensure that no moisture is captured inside the case. The most

Restoring a Napoleonic prisoner-of-war ship model

This illustration shows an early stage in any restoration – an exhaustive survey of all breakages and losses. The severely damaged upper masts are held erect by delicately balanced counter-weights, suspended above the model.

Bone and pine, French, early 19th century, 30.5cm (12in) long

vulnerable part of a ship model is the rigging which, in the case of prisoner-of-war models, is sometimes made from human hair, but more usually twine. These organic materials will deteriorate with time and the model will appear as though it has been through a hurricane, with the masts and spars awry and rigging hanging loose. This should only be repaired by an expert, as many models have been ruined by amateurs trying to replace rigging.

Instruments

All metal instruments should be carefully handled, since the salts and acids contained in the moisture of the human skin can leave a permanent fingerprint on the metal surface. Sodium chloride, lactic acid and amino and fatty acids are corrosive to copper alloys and steel, and damage can be prevented by the wearing of either cotton or surgical gloves. Rubber gloves should not be used, as they sometimes contain sulphides which also act as a corrosive.

It is very important to try to maintain, where possible, the original lacquer finish to brass, which would have been applied to the surface as a means of protection. Clear lacquer was especially useful as a means of detering corrosion to scales, and other parts, where engraving needed to be seen clearly. An example is the silver scale of a sextant which, if exposed to the atmosphere, oxidizes and turns black, making a reading almost impossible. With age, the lacquer takes on a rich dark hue which adds to the patina of the surface and indicates that an instrument has seen little use and should, therefore, be in good original condition. For this reason, the lay person should not attempt to clean brass other than by careful dusting, and collectors should be wary of instruments that have been cleaned either by the use of metal polish, or by dipping in an acidic solution, as the lacquer will have been stripped away.

Lacquering can be replaced, and modern lacquer, which is based on cellulose nitrate, gives a good effect, although is still possible to distinguish it from old lacquer. Professional restorers can make up a traditional lacquer using ingredients of gum and resin and this is applied using a brush or spray. To ensure a covering of uniform thickness takes great skill and should be left to an expert. Similarly, great care should also be taken when dealing with scientific instruments made from gilded brass, as incorrect handling will remove the thin surface layer of gold.

Instruments such as wooden octants and quadrants, which combine organic constituents, such as ebony or rosewood, with ivory or boxwood scales, require careful storage and display. Dry conditions, aggravated by modern central heating, can have devastating effects on instruments, such as distortion, shrinkage and cracking. Wide fluctuations in relative humidity and temperature, if repeated often enough, will certainly cause instruments to crack and break, and it is suggested, therefore, that the atmosphere be kept at a constant temperature of 18°C (64°F.) with a relative humidity of 55 per cent, plus or minus 3 per cent. For the illumination of a display case and its contents, a maximum of 150 lux is safe for the majority of organic substances.

When buying a chronometer, it is important to note whether the movement is working and keeping good time, and to enquire if it has been restored. A professional restorer will, where possible, use original materials. However, for the movement to work, it is sometimes necessary to have some parts replaced, and such replacements might well have a detrimental effect on the value. Moreover, chronometer movements are delicate and should not be touched by the lay person, since any 'bodging' can cause extensive damage and eventual cost. The oiling, cleaning and general overhauling of the movement should be undertaken by a professional chronometer movement restorer and not the local watch repairer. Maintenance should also be carried out on a regular basis, rather than waiting until the movement stops, which may impose strain on certain elements of the mechanism.

Mercury barometers

Barometers should be handled and moved very carefully, since a sudden jolt, or placing the instrument at a horizontal angle, can cause the mercury to leak. In addition to being extremely difficult to collect, once spilt, mercury is highly poisonous and very corrosive to certain metals.

Globes

The spheres of globes were usually composed of a wooden skeleton inside a rigid shell of papier-mâché, with an outer coating of plaster. The paper maps, or gores, were printed flat, sometimes hand-coloured, and then cut out and pasted on to the sphere. Large floor-standing library globes are, by nature, a tactile form of furniture and, for the uninformed, there is a great temptation to spin the globe. Such treatment will stress the pivots and discolour the paper surface. Restoration to the structure of a globe, and to the paper, can be a long and costly process, since the gores have to be carefully removed from the sphere and cleaned, the sphere structure repaired, and the gores subsequently reapplied to the surface. In view of the expense of such a highly specialized operation, the cost of any necessary repair should be borne in mind when purchasing a globe.

Wool-work pictures

Wool-work pictures should always be displayed in relatively dark conditions, since strong light will cause the dyes in the wool to fade. The picture should be glazed, to prevent the surface being attacked by moisture, smoke or insects, and stretched over an acid-free surface. This surface, perhaps of washed linen, should be mounted on special conservation board which, together with the original wooden stretcher, is non-acidic, and will not attack the cloth. The back of the frame should be carefully sealed to prevent dampness or insects from entering. Moth damage is often evident on wool-work pictures and any replacement to large areas of the embroidery can only be successfully achieved by a professional restorer. Again, all textiles should be kept at a constant humidity and temperature, in order to prevent the threads drying out and becoming brittle.

Oil paintings, watercolours and drawings

For the structure of a painting to remain stable, it is important that the environment in which it is housed is kept at a uniform temperature and humidity. The worst possible place for hanging a painting is over a fireplace where the smoke, heat and dust will quickly deteriorate the canvas. Over a period of time, canvases will get torn and dented and, in the event of major damage, will have to be re-lined. This involves mounting the painting on to a second piece of canvas to give it strength, and to enable the area of the tear to be supported and allow any paint flakes to be secured. However, if this re-lining process is undertaken inexpertly, it can be potentially damaging to the picture.

Oil paintings can also be cleaned sometimes with outstanding results, as what appeared to be a dull painting is revealed from under years of hidden grime. However, all such cleaning and restoration of the paintwork should be dealt with by a professional.

Prior to the early nineteenth century, watercolours and drawings were normally housed in folders rather than being hung on a wall, since the glass necessary to protect the picture was very expensive. Works of art on paper are susceptible to two main problems: the fading of the coloured pigments, and the deterioration of the paper. When buying such a piece, the condition of both elements should be considered, since restoration by a professional could well be long and expensive.

It is imperative, therefore, when undertaking any restoration on a work of art, to use an experienced and sympathetic conservator or restorer, and to ensure that the work is both detectable and reversible. Any restoration which is irreversible, defaces a piece, and will make any future work much more difficult to complete satisfactorily.

Marine Collections open to the Public

AUSTRALIA

Adelaide

South Australian Maritime Museum,
126 Lipson St, Port Adelaide, SA 5015
Telephone: 240 0200
Opening Times: Tuesday to Sunday 1000-1700
Collection: Large site displaying full-size vessels, together with figureheads, immigration artefacts and ephemera.
Location: In Port Adelaide on the quay at Port River.

Sydney

The Australian National Maritime Museum, Sydney, NSW
Telephone: 612 552 7777
Opening Times: Daily 1000-1700
Collection: A varied collection of paintings, posters, furniture, figureheads and marine arts relating to Australian history and culture.
Location: At Darling Harbour, an arm of Sydney Harbour adjoining the central business district.

CANADA

Halifax

Maritime Command Museum, Admiralty House, CFB Halifax
Telephone: 902 427 4077
Opening Times: September to June, weekdays 0930-1530; July and August, Monday to Friday 0930-2030, Saturday and Sunday 1300-1700
Collection: Archives and library relating to the Navy in Halifax since 1759, and a predominantly twentieth-century collection of exhibits relating to Canada's maritime military forces.

Vancouver

The Vancouver Maritime Museum, Vancouver, British Columbia
Telephone: 604 737 2211
Opening Times: Daily 1000-1700
Collection: The Naval and Merchant Service, history and trade of British Columbia with exhibits of navigation, ship models, figureheads, paintings and photographic archive.

DENMARK

Copenhagen

Royal Danish Naval Museum,
Overgaden Oven Vandet 58, Copenhagen
Telephone: 45 31 546363
Opening Times: Check with museum
Collection: Fine collection of eighteenth-century dockyard models, marine paintings, figureheads and Royal barges.

Helsingør

The Danish Maritime Museum, Kronborg Castle, 3000 Helsingør
Telephone: 49 21 06 85
Opening Times: May to September, daily 1030-1700; April to October, daily 1100 -1600; November to March, daily 1100-1500
Collection: Exhibits illustrating the history of Danish shipping and the trade with her colonies, together with a large collection of ship models, paintings, drawings and an extensive library.
Location: Kronborg Castle has for over 400 years been a Danish landmark due to its prominent position overlooking the Sound.

FINLAND

Mariehamn

The Åland Maritime Museum, Hamngaten 2, Mariehamn

Telephone: 928 11 930

Opening Times: Daily 1000-1600, late closing in the summer months.

Collection: Based on the marine collection of Captain Carl Holmqvist, the museum displays are housed in a ship setting with models, portraits, instruments, log books and a wide range of nineteenth- and twentieth-century ships' furnishings and fittings.

FRANCE

Paris

Musée de la Marine, Palais de Chaillot, Paris

Telephone: 45 53 31 70

Opening Times: Daily 1000-1800

Collection: National Maritime Museum with a wide range of fine and decorative ship models, Napoleon's barge, marine paintings, figureheads and other nautical works of art.

Location: Nearest metro: Trocadero.

Marseille

Marseille Museum of Maritime and Economic Affairs, Palaise de la Bourse, Marseilles

Telephone: 91 91 91 51

Collection: A permanent exhibition of the Maritime history of this important Mediterranean port, including many paintings by the Roux family, ship models, navigational instruments, twentieth-century ocean liner memorabilia, and displays of underwater technology and marine archaeology.

Location: On the quayside.

GERMANY

Bremerhaven

German Museum of Shipping and Navigation, van Ronzelen Strasse, 27568 Bremerhaven

Telephone: 471 482 070

Opening Times: Tuesday to Sunday 1000-1800, closed Mondays.

Collection: Exhibition of the history of shipping and navigation, including ship models and many full-size period vessels.

Location: On the quayside.

Hamburg

Altonaer Museum in Hamburg, Museumstrasse 23, 22765 Hamburg

Telephone: 3 80 74 83

Opening Times: Daily 1000-1700

Collection: An exhibition of shipping and navigation, including the fishing industry of the North German ports, a good collection of figureheads and other marine artefacts.

Location: All S-Bahn lines to station Altona.

Munich

Deutsches Museum, Museumsinsel, 80538 München

Telephone: 89 21791

Opening Times: Daily 0900-1700, closed on public holidays.

Collection: National museum of natural sciences and technology, including shipbuilding and navigation.

Location: All S-Bahn lines to Isartor, U-Bahn lines 1 and 2 to Fraunhofer, tram 18 to Deutsches Museum. Limited local parking.

GREAT BRITAIN

Aberdeen

Aberdeen Maritime Museum, Provost Ross's House, Shiprow, Aberdeen, Grampian
Telephone: 0224 585788
Opening Times: Monday to Saturday 1000-1700
Collection: Fishing boat models, works of art and painting relating to local shipping industry and North Sea Oil.
Location: Central Aberdeen.

Arlington

Arlington Court, Arlington, Barnstable, Devon, EX31 4LP
Telephone: 027850 296
Opening Times: April to October, Sunday to Friday 1100-1730
Collection: An important collection of thirty-six prisoner-of-war ship models housed in a National Trust house.
Location: Off the A39 Barnstable to Lynton road.

Bamburgh

Grace Darling Museum, 1, Radcliffe Rd, Bamburgh, Northumberland, NE69 7AE
Telephone: 0665 720037
Opening Times: Check by telephone.
Collection: Memorabilia relating to Grace Darling, the lighthouse keeper's daughter, who achieved great fame in 1838, when she rescued the crew of the merchant ship *Forfarshire* which was wrecked on the Farne Islands.

Beaulieu

Buckler's Hard Village, Beaulieu, Hampshire
Telephone: 0590613 203
Opening Times: All year, except Christmas Day 1000-1630, later during summer months.
Collection: Museum portraying the history of Buckler's Hard as a shipbuilding centre, especially for the building of many ships from Nelson's fleet, including HMS *Agamemnon*. Includes: ship models, original drawings, artefacts and dioramas.
Location: On the Beaulieu River, near the village of Beaulieu.

Belfast

Ulster Museum, Botanic Gardens, Belfast, BT9 5AB
Telephone: 0232 381251
Opening Times: Weekdays 1000-1700, Saturday 1300-1700, Sunday 1400-1700
Collection: Museum of fine, applied and decorative arts, industrial technology and archaeology. Marine section includes relics from the Armarda wrecked on local shores.
Location: On the south side of city.

Bembridge

The Maritime Museum, Bembridge, Isle of Wight, PO35 5SB
Telephone: 0983 873125
Opening Times: Easter to October, daily 1000-1700
Collection: Permanent exhibition of ship models, navigation, shipwrecks, early diving equipment, the story of the hovercraft and paddle-steamers.
Location: In the centre of the village.

Bideford

North Devon Maritime Museum, Odun House, Appledore, Bideford, Devon, EX39 1PT
Telephone: 0237 471455
Opening Times: Easter to end of September, daily 1400-1730
Collection: History of north Devon's shipping industry.
Location: Located in the village of Appledore, Odun Rd is off the main hill into the village.

Birkenhead

Williamson Museum & Art Gallery, Slatey Rd, Birkenhead, Wirral, L43 4UE
Telephone: 051 652 4177
Opening Times: Monday to Saturday 1000-1700, Sunday 1400-1700
Collection: Collection of Cammell Laird shipbuilders' models and photographic archive.
Location: From M53 take Woodchurch exit towards Birkenhead and follow signs to Williamson Art Gallery.

Bristol

SS *Great Britain*, Great Western Dock,
Gas Ferry Rd, Bristol, Avon, BS1 6TY

Telephone: 0272 260680

Opening Times: Summer, daily 1000-1800;
Winter, daily 1000-1700

Collection: The preservation and restoration
project of Brunel's first ocean-going, propeller-
driven iron ship. Collection of models and
drawings illustrating the history of Bristol
shipbuilding.

Location: Follow signs from city centre.

Cardiff

Welsh Industrial and Maritime Museum, Bute St,
Docks, Cardiff, South Glamorgan, CF1 CAM

Telephone: 0222 481919

Opening Times: Tuesday to Saturday 1000-1700,
Sunday 1430-1700, closed on public holidays.

Collection: Display of maritime history in Wales
over the last 200 years.

Location: Bute St is the south bound road out of
the city.

Castletown

The Nautical Museum, Castletown, Isle of Man

Telephone: 0624 75522

Opening Times: May to September, Monday to
Sunday 1000-1700

Collection: Well-preserved example of the
eighteenth-century schooner-rigged yacht, *Peggy*,
in boathouse. Display of the nautical life of the
Isle of Man.

Location: Bridge St, Umber Quay of the harbour.

Chatham

Chatham Historic Dockyard Trust, Old Pay Office,
Church Lane, Chatham Historic Dockyard,
Chatham, Kent, ME4 4TE

Telephone: 0634 812551

Opening Times: April to October, Wednesday to
Sunday and Bank Holidays 1000-1800; November
to March, Wednesday, Saturday and Sunday
1000-1630

Collection: Chatham was the principal
shipbuilding yard in the early seventeenth
century. A Royal dockyard from the time of Henry
VIII to 1984, this very large site contains
Georgian and Victorian listed buildings, together
with a collection of naval ordnance, working
ropery, mast house and other dockyard industries.

Location: A2 to Chatham centre, A231 to
Gillingham, then follow signs.

Dartmouth

Dartmouth Museum, The Butterwalk, Dartmouth,
Devon, TQ6 9PZ

Telephone: 08043 2923

Opening Times: Summer, daily 1100-1700;
Winter, daily 1415-1600

Collection: Located in a seventeenth-century
merchantman's house. Collection includes: the
development of ship design, paintings and
photographic archive.

Location: Centre of town.

Edinburgh

Royal Museum of Scotland, Chambers St,
Edinburgh, EH1 1JF

Telephone: 031 225 7534

Opening Times: Monday to Saturday 1000-1700,
Sunday 1200-1700

Collection: National collection of decorative and
applied arts. Comprehensive collection of
navigational instruments and chronometers,
shipbuilders' models and prisoner-of-war models.

Location: From Princess St, first turning on right
on George IV Bridge.

Exeter

Exeter Maritime Museum, 60 Haven Rd, Exeter, Devon, EX2 8TD

Telephone: 0392 58075

Opening Times: June to September, daily 1000-1700; October to May, daily 1000-1600

Collection: Large collection of working crafts and boats. Located in large building with many vessels floating on the canal.

Location: City centre, follow signs.

Falmouth

Falmouth Maritime Museum, Bell's Court, Falmouth, Cornwall

Telephone: 0326 250 507

Opening Times: Daily 1000-1600, except Christmas holiday period.

Collection: A display of the history of shipping in Cornwall.

Location: Town centre, off Market Square.

Glasgow

Glasgow Museum of Transport, Kelvin Hall, 1, Bunhouse Rd, Glasgow, G3 8DP

Telephone: 041 357 3929

Opening Times: Monday to Saturday 1000-1700, Sunday 1100-1700

Collection: Important collection of shipbuilders' models and displays outlining the history of Clyde shipbuilding.

Location: Follow signs from city centre.

Great Yarmouth

Maritime Museum for East Anglia, Marine Parade, Great Yarmoth, Norfolk, NR30 2EN

Telephone: 0493 842267

Opening Times: Summer, Sunday to Friday 1000-1730; winter, Sunday to Friday 1000-1300 and 1400-1730

Collection: Displays on the early life of Nelson, the Norfolk Broads, merchant and naval shipping, plans and contemporary photographs.

Location: On seafront parade.

Greenock

McLean Museum and Art Gallery, 15 Kelly St, Greenock, Strathcylde, PA16 8JX

Telephone: 0475 23741

Opening Times: Monday to Saturday 1000-1200 and 1300-1700

Collection: Collection of ship models and marine paintings.

Location: Town centre.

Grimsby

Alexandra Dock, Grimsby, South Humberside, DN31 1UF

Telephone: 0472 344867

Opening Times: Monday to Sunday 1000-1700, closed on public holidays.

Collection: Good collection of shipbuilders' models, prisoner-of-war models, together with navigational instruments, contemporary photographs and other marine artefacts.

Location: Follow signs from city centre.

Hartlepool

Hartlepool Maritime Museum, Northgate Hartlepool, Cleveland, TS24 0LP

Telephone: 0429 272814

Opening Times: Monday to Saturday 1000-1700, closed on public holidays

Collection: Collection of ship plans, marine engineering records, ship models and marine artefacts.

Location: Two miles from the centre of town, at Hartlepool Headland.

Irvine

Scottish Maritime Museum, Laird Forge, Gottries Rd, Irvine, Ayrshire, KA12 8QE

Telephone: 0294 78283

Opening Times: Summer, daily 1000-1700

Collection: Display of local maritime history, restoration workshops and full-size vessels.

Location: Irvine Central, Harbour side.

Kingston-upon-Hull

Town Docks Museum, Queen Victoria Square, Hull, North Humberside, HU1 3DX

Telephone: 0482 593902

Opening Times: Monday to Saturday 1000-1700, Sunday 1330-1630

Collection: History of the whaling and shipbuilding industries of Hull, depicted by models, scrimshaw and contemporary photographs.

Location: City centre.

Lancaster

Lancaster Maritime Museum, Custom House, St George's Quay, Lancaster, Lancashire, LA1 1RB

Telephone: 0524 64637

Opening Times: Summer, daily 1000-1700; Winter, daily 1400-1700

Collection: Ship models from the nineteenth and twentieth centuries, including the fishing industry in Morecombe Bay.

Location: West bank of the river Lune.

Liverpool

Merseyside Maritime Museum, Albert Dock, Liverpool, L3 4AA

Telephone: 051 207 0001

Opening Times: Daily 1030-1730

Collection: Important collection relating to the flourishing merchant shipping business in Liverpool during the nineteenth and twentieth centuries. Shipbuilders' models, the Pilkington collection of prisoner-of-war boxwood ship models, histoy of emigration from Liverpool, posters, ships' fittings and a collection of marine paintings by well-known local artists.

Location: Follow signs for Liverpool Pierhead.

London

National Maritime Museum, Romney Rd, Greenwich, London, SE10 9NF

Telephone: 081 858 4422

Opening Times: Summer, Monday to Saturday 1000-1800, Sunday 1200-1800; winter, Monday to Saturday 1000-1700, Sunday 1400-1700

Collection: National collections of important maritime and astronomical artefacts and paintings. Marine section housed in the main buildings, while astronomical and horological exhibits are housed at the top of the hill where the Old Royal Observatory is located. Collection includes: highly important and early chronometers, telescopes, astrolabes and other navigational and astronomical instruments; shipbuilders' and superb dockyard models and prisoner-of-war models; ships' fittings, figureheads, maritime archaeology and full-size vessels; an extensive permanent and travelling exhibitions on specific nautical themes; belongings of famous seamen, including Nelson's Trafalgar uniform; collection of swords, firearms and guns for sea service and history of naval uniforms; charts, atlases and globes, printed books and manuscripts; highly important marine paintings from the sixteenth century to the present day; historic photograph archive and other nautical works of art.

Location: East of central London, good connections by train, bus and water bus from Charing Cross, London Bridge, St Catherine's Dock and Canary Wharf.

Science Museum, Exhibition Rd, London, SW7 2DD

Telephone: 071 938 8000

Opening Times: Monday to Saturday 1000-1800, Sunday 1430-1800, closed on public holidays.

Collection: Important collection of ship models, marine steam engines, boilers, turbines and auxiliary machinery.

Location: Near South Kensington Underground station.

The National Maritime Museum, Greenwich, England

The Queen's House, flanked by the two wings of the National Maritime Museum, with the Royal Observatory in the background.

Lowestoft

Lowestoft Maritime Museum, Sparrows Nest Park, Whaplode Rd, Lowestoft, Suffolk

Telephone: 0502 561963

Opening Times: May to September 1000-1700

Collection: Display of east coast fishing vessel models, lifeboat models and coastguard equipment; sailors' and fishermen's tools and effects; and a collection of marine paintings.

Location: Near the Lowestoft High Lighthouse.

Maryport

Maritime Museum, 1, Shipping Brow, Senhouse St, Maryport, Cumbria, CA15 6AB

Telephone: 0900 813738

Opening Times: Monday to Saturday 1000-1700, Sunday 1400-1700

Collection: Full-size vessels, preserved in harbour and museum, displaying the history of shipping on the Solway Firth. Shipbuilding, fishing, sail-making and other ancillary industries located in and around Maryport are described in detail.

Location: Harbour side.

Middlesbrough

Captain Cook Birthplace Museum, Stewart Park, Marton, Middlesbrough, Cleveland, TS7 6AS

Telephone: 0642 311211

Opening Times: Summer, daily 1000-1730; winter, daily 0900-1600

Collection: Display of personal relics and models relating to the life of Captain Cook.

Location: Follow signs from the A172.

Newcastle-upon-Tyne

Museum of Science and Engineering, Blandford House, Blandford St, Newcastle-upon-Tyne, NE1 4JA

Telephone: 091 2326789

Opening Times: Tuesday to Friday 1000-1730, Saturday 1000-1630

Collection: Museum devoted to the history of Tyneside shipping from 1880 to 1930, including fine shipbuilders' models, plans and photographs. A collection of marine paintings, prisoner-of-war models, navigational instruments, ship and engine models is also on display.

Location: City centre.

Peterborough

Peterborough City Art Gallery and Museum, Priestgate, Peterborough, PE1 1LF

Telephone: 0733 43329

Opening Times: Tuesday to Saturday 1000-1700, Bank Holiday Monday 1000-1700

Collection: Important collection of Napoleonic prisoner-of-war work, mainly made at the local prison, Norman Cross, including straw work, bone models and other artefacts.

Location: On the inner ring road between junctions with the A1 and A15.

Plymouth

Plymouth City Museum and Art Gallery, Drake Circus, Plymouth, Devon, PL4 8AJ

Telephone: 0752 264979

Opening Times: Tuesday to Saturday 1000-1700, Bank Holiday Monday 1000-1700

Collection: Marine paintings and ship models together with a more general decorative and fine art collection.

Location: City centre.

Portsmouth

Mary Rose Ship Hall and Exhibition, Building 110, College Rd, HM Naval Base, Portsmouth, Hampshire, PO1 3LX

Telephone: 0705 750521

Opening Times: Summer, daily 1000-1730; winter, daily 1000-1700

Collection: Mary Rose was Henry VIII's warship built at Portsmouth in 1510-11. It sank in the Solent and was excavated and raised in 1982. The remains are now on display, together with artefacts from the excavation and reconstructions of parts of the ship.

Location: Signposted from city centre.

Royal Naval Museum, HM Naval Base, Portsmouth, Hampshire, PO1 3LR

Telephone: 0705 822351

Opening Times: Daily 1030-1700

Collection: Large site with access to the HMS *Victory* and HMS *Warrior*, includes three storehouses with exhibitions of the history of the Royal Navy from the time of the *Mary Rose* to the present day, together with collections of medals, Nelson commemorative wares, ship models, paintings and relics.

Location: Follow signs from city centre.

Sunderland

Sunderland Museum and Art Gallery, Borough Rd, Sunderland, SR1 1PP

Telephone: 091 514 1235

Opening Times: Tuesday to Friday 1000-1730, Saturday 1000-1600, Sunday 1400-1700

Collection: Exhibition of local merchant shipping industries including a large collection of shipbuilders' models, including the Doxford Yard, marine paintings by local artists.

Location: At the crossroads of A690 and A1016.

Topsham

Topsham Museum., 25 The Strand, Topsham, Devon, EX3 0AX

Telephone: 039 287 3244

Opening Times: February to November, Monday, Wednesday and Saturday 1400-1700

Collection: History of the Topsham as a port and Holman's as a shipyard. Displays include: ship models, figureheads, tools, paintings and photographs.

Location: In main street.

Yelverton

Buckland Abbey, Nr Yelverton, Devon

Telephone: 0822 853607

Opening Times: Summer, weekdays 1100-1800, Sunday 1400-1800; winter, Wednesday, Saturday, Sunday 1400-1700

Collection: House that was once owned by Sir Francis Drake with displays of Drake mementoes and Drake's Drum. Now owned by the National Trust.

Location: Off A386 between Crownhill and Yelverton.

ITALY

Venice

Museo Storico Navale, Riva San Biagio, Venice

Telephone: 41 5200276

Opening Times: Monday to Saturday 0900-1300

Collection: Display of the story of Venice's maritime history and Italian maritime power.

Location: Riva San Biago near the Arsenale, Waterbus Line 1 land at Arsenale, Waterbus Line 5 land at Tana.

THE NETHERLANDS

Amsterdam

Scheepvaartmuseum, Kattenburgerplein 1,
1018 KK Amsterdam

Telephone: 20 52 32 222

Opening Times: Tuesday to Saturday 1000-1700,
Sunday and public holidays 1200-1700; 15 June
to 15 September on Monday 1000-1700

Collection: One of the largest and most important
collections, providing a chronological survey of
Dutch maritime history. The principal topics
include: overseas trade, naval wars, fishery, inland
shipping, navigation and cartography.

Location: Bus 22 or 28 from Central Station.

Rotterdam

Maritiem Museum Prince Hendrik, Leuvehaven 1,
3011 EA, Rotterdam

Telephone: 413 26 80

Opening Times: Thursday to Saturday 1000-1700,
Sunday and public holidays 1100-1700

Collection: A general collection of Dutch maritime
history with an emphasis on Rotterdam and
hinterland, including ship models, paintings,
prints, posters, navigational instruments, maps
and atlases, technical drawings and photographs.

Location: City centre.

NORWAY

Horten

The Royal Norwegian Navy Museum, POB 21,
3191 Horten

Telephone: 47 33 42 081

Opening Times: Monday to Friday 1000-1500,
Sunday 1200-1600; May to October on Saturday
1200-1600

Collection: History of the Norwegian Navy from
the mid-nineteenth century to the present day.

Location: Magazine A at the old naval base,
Karljohansvern.

Oslo

Norsk Sjofartsmuseum, Bygdoynesveien 37,
Oslo 2

Telephone: 2 55 63 95

Opening Times: 15 April to 30 September, daily
1030-2000; 1 October to 14 April, daily 1030-
1600

Collection: The national collection of maritime
history and culture.

Location: Bus 30 from city centre, or by ferry from
pier C.

PORTUGAL

Lisbon

Museu de Marinha, Praco do Imperio, Lisbon

Telephone: 351 1 3620032

Opening Times: Tuesday to Sunday 1000-1700

Collection: Displays of models of Portuguese ships
from the fifteenth century to the present day,
including Royal galleys, charts, uniforms and
navigational instruments.

Location: West wing of the Monastery of
Jeronimos, Belem.

SPAIN

Barcelona

Museu Maritim, Drassanes Reials,
Porta de la Pau 1, 08001 Barcelona

Telephone: 301 18 71

Opening Times: Tuesday to Saturday 0930-1300,
1600-1900; Sunday 1000-1400

Collection: Important collection of ship models,
late nineteenth- and early twentieth-century
Catalan paintings, navigational instruments,
figureheads and full-size ships.

Location: Housed in the Royal Dockyards at the
end of the Rambla near the Port.

SWEDEN

Karlskrona

Swedish Naval Museum (Marinmuseum),
S-37130 Karlskrona
Telephone: 455 86241
Opening Times: Daily 1200-1600.
Collection: The museum was established in 1752
as a Chamber of Models and contains an important
collection of ship models, shipbuilders' tools and
figureheads from the period 1770-1880, together
with light arms, steam engines and
telecommunications from 1840.

Gothenburg

Maritime Museum, Karl-Johansgatan 1-3,
S-414 59 Goteborg
Telephone: 31 611000
Opening Times: September to April 0900-1600,
Saturday and Sunday 1000 -1700, Wednesday
0900-2100; May to August, Monday to Friday
0900-1600, Saturday and Sunday 1000-1700
Collection: An important collection of figureheads
and other carved wood ships' decorations. There
are also displays of the maritime trade to and from
Gothenburg during the nineteenth and twentieth
centuries.
Location: City centre.

Stockholm

National Maritime Museum,
Djurgardsbrunnsvagen 24, S-102 52, Stockholm
Telephone: 8 666 49 00
Opening Times: Daily 1000-1700
Collection: An important collection of over 1,500
ship models and 500 ship portraits, together with
navigational instruments, figureheads, stern
boards and other fixtures and fittings.
Location: 2km from city centre.

UNITED STATES OF AMERICA

Annapolis

U.S. Naval Academy Museum, 118 Maryland Ave,
Annapolis, Maryland
Telephone: 301 267 2108
Opening Times: Monday to Saturday 0900-1700,
Sunday 1100-1700
Collection: The Rogers ship model collection is
one of the most important collections of dockyard
models in the world, and many are now displayed
in a new gallery. Exhibits also include paintings,
prints, flags, uniforms, books, models and other
collections relating to the history of the U.S. Navy.
Location: In Preble Hall on the grounds of the U.S.
Naval Academy.

Boston

The Boston Historical Society and Museum,
Old State House, 206 Washington St, Boston,
Massachusetts, MA 02109
Telephone: 617 720 1713
Opening Times: Daily 0900-1700
Collection: Maritime history of Boston, including
figureheads, scrimshaw, paintings and prints,
posters and ceramics.
Location: City centre.

Mystic

Mystic Seaport Museum, 50 Greenmanville Ave,
Mystic, Connecticut, CT 06355-0990
Telephone: 203 572-0711
Opening Times: April to mid-June, daily 0900-
1700; mid-June to September, daily 0900-2000;
September to October, daily 0900-1700;
November to March, daily 0900-1600
Collection: America's largest maritime museum set
out on seventeen acres with preserved shipyard,
stores and ship related buildings. Many full-size
vessels, together with ship models, figureheads,
scrimshaw, paintings, photographs and
navigational instruments, are on display.
Location: From Interstate 95, take exit 90 and
follow 'Seaport' signs for one mile along Route 27.

Mystic Seaport, Mystic, Connecticut, U.S.A.

A horse and carriage passes in
front of the 1841 *Charles W
Morgan*, the last wooden whaler, at
Mystic Seaport. In the background
is the Danish training vessel,
Joseph Conrad, built in 1882.
Mystic Seaport is an indoor and
outdoor museum dedicated to
preserving American maritime
heritage.

Nantucket

Nantucket Whaling Museum, Broad St,
Nantucket, Massachusetts, MA 02554

Telephone: 508 228 1894

Opening Times: In season, daily 1000-1700

Collection: Housed in a former factory for refining
whale oils, the collection includes: a whaleboat,
the tools used in whaling and portraits of the
island's whalemen.

Location: Near the steamboat wharf.

Newport, Rhode Island

Newport Historical Society, 82 Touro St, Newport,
Rhode Island, RI 02840

Telephone: 401 846 0813

Opening Times: Check with museum.

Collection: A maritime history of Newport in the
form of portraits, navigational instruments,
scrimshaw, tools and manuscripts.

Newport News, Virginia

The Mariners' Museum, 100 Museum Drive,
Newport News, Virginia, VA 23606-3759

Telephone: 804 595 0386

Opening Times: Monday to Saturday 0900-1700,
Sunday 1200-1700

Collection: America's most extensive international
collection of marine paintings, maps, scrimshaw,
coins, ship models and unique watercraft.

Location: Between Williamsburg and Virginia
Beach, Norfolk, off Route 64, exit 258A.

New York

South Street Seaport Museum, 207 Front St,
New York, NY 10038

Telephone: 212 669 9424 (recorded info.); 212
669 9400 (museum offices)

Opening Times: Daily 1000-1700

Collection: A changing exhibition illustrating New
York's growth from fur-trading post to booming
city. Set in a large site by Pier 16, it contains
many full-size nineteenth- and early twentieth-
century vessels, craft centres, shops, restaurants
and galleries.

Location: Nearest subway stations are Fulton
Street, Broadway-Nassau and World Trade Centre.

Philadelphia

Philadelphia Maritime Museum, 321 Chesnut St,
Philadelphia, Pennsylvania, PA 19106

Telephone: 215 925 5439

Opening Times: Check with museum.

Collection: A permanent exhibition of ship models,
figureheads, paintings, prints, arms and other
maritime wares relating to the port of
Philadelphia.

Salem

Peabody & Essex Museum, East India Square,
Salem, Massachusetts, MA 01970

Telephone: 508 745 1876

Opening Times: Monday to Saturday 1000-1700,
Sunday 1200-1700

Collection: A display of ship models, paintings,
figureheads and the arts and tools of the shipping
trade.

San Francisco

San Francisco Maritime Museum, Fort Museum,
San Francisco, California, CA 94123

Telephone: 415 556 3002

Opening Times: Daily 1000-1700

Collection: A large site with full-size historic
vessels moored at several piers. The museum
houses several collections of whaling exhibits,
steamship technology, figureheads and the history
of West Coast shipping.

Location: Adjacent to Fisherman's Wharf.

Washington, D.C.

The Smithsonian Institution, 14th St and
Constitution Ave. N.W., Washington, D.C. 20560

Telephone: 202 357 1300

Opening Times: Daily 1000-1700

Collection: The maritime historical collections are
shared among several of the museums on the Mall,
with the vast majority concentrated at the National
Museum of American History. The collection here
includes: important ship models, ship portraits,
scrimshaw, a complete engine room and other
ships' fittings and furnishings.

Location: Central Washington museum area.

Bibliography

Bailey, S. F.
   Cutty Sark Figureheads (London, 1992)
Baldwin, Robert
   Globes (London, 1992)
Bennett, James A.
   The Divided Circle (London, 1987)
Brewington, M. V.
   *The Peabody Museum Collection of Navigating
   Instruments* (Salem, Massachusetts)
Cary, Alan L.
   *Famous Liners and Their Stories; Giant Liners of
   the World* (London, 1937)
Eastland, Jonathan
   Great Yachts and their Designers
   (London, 1987)
Finch, Roger
   *The Pierhead Painter, Naïve Ship Portrait
   Painters 1750-1950* (London, 1983)
Flayderman, E. Norman
   *Scrimshaw and Scrimshanders, Whales and
   Whalemen,* (New Milford, Connecticut, 1972)
Franklin, John
   Navy Board Ship Models 1650-1750
   (London, 1989)
Freestone, Ewart C.
   Prisoner-of-War Ship Models 1775-1825
   (Lymington, 1973)
Frere-Cook, Gervis
   The Decorative Arts of the Mariner
   (London, 1966)
Fuller, Roland
   The Bassett-Lowke Story (London, 1984)
Goodison, Nicholas
   English Barometers 1680-1860
   (Woodbridge, 1977)
Hansen, H. J.
   *Art and the Seafarer, A Historical Survey of the
   Arts and Crafts of Sailors and Shipwrights*
   (London, 1968)
Hansen, H. J. and C. B.
   Ships' Figureheads
   (West Chester, Pennsylvania, 1990)
Johnson, Peter
   The Encyclopaedia of Yachting (London, 1989)
Keble-Chatterton, E.
   Steamship Models, (London, 1924)
Kemp, Peter (ed.)
   The Oxford Companion to Ships & The Sea
   (London, 1976)

Landstrom, Bjorn
   The Ship (London, 1961)
Lavery, Brian
   The Ship of the Line (London, 1983)
   *Nelson's Navy, The Ships, Men and
   Organization 1793-1815* (London, 1989)
   *Lloyd Collection of Napoleonic Prisoner of War
   Artefacts,* exh. cat., Kennebunkport Maritime
   Museum, Maine, 1986
Maber, John M.
   The Ship, Channel Packets and Ocean Liners
   (London, 1980)
Norton, Peter J.
   Ships' Figureheads (London, 1976)
Pugh, P. D. Gordon
   Naval Ceramics (Newport, Rhode Island, 1971)
Randier, Jean
   L'Objet de Marine (Paris, 1992)
   Nautical Antiques for the Collector
   (London, 1976)
Simpson, Mette and Huntley, Michael (eds)
   Caring for Antiques (London, 1992)
Stephens, Simon
   Ship Models (London, 1992)
Stevenson, Edward Luther
   Terrestrial and Celestial Globes (London, 1921)
Taylor, David
   Figureheads (London, 1992)
Turner, Gerard L'E.
   Antique Scientific Instruments (Poole, 1980)
   Nineteeth Century Scientific Instruments
   (London, 1983)
Van der Krogt, Peter
   Old Globes in the Netherlands (Utrecht, 1984)
   Visual Dictionary of Ships and Sailing
   (London, 1991)
Waite, A. H.
   *National Maritime Museum Catalogue of Ship
   Models, Part 1 Ships of the Western Tradition to
   1815* (London)
Willams, G. R.
   The World of Model Ships and Boats
   (London, 1971)
Wilson, T.
   Flags at Sea (London, 1986)
Wynter, Harriet and Turner, Antony
   Scientific Instruments (London, 1975)

Photographic Acknowledgements

Grateful acknowledgement is due to the following for supplying copyright photographic material and for permission to reproduce it.
Numerals are page numbers, italics indicating reproductions in colour.

Beken of Cowes p.131
Christie's pp.19, *81* top left, *117*, 121, 122, *129* bottom
Jonathan Tatlow p.140
Mystic Seaport, Mystic, Connecticut (photo: Mary Anne Stets) p.153
National Maritime Museum pp.*8*, *13*, *17* bottom, *68*, *69*, *104*, *105*, *109*, *132*, *136* right, 149
Onslow's Auctioneers pp.135, *136* left, *137*, 138

All remaining photographic material was supplied from Sotheby's

Index